Special Thanks

To my **Lord and Savior Jesus Christ**, You made all of this possible. My sincere gratitude goes to James Wing for his tireless service of love for the Lord in helping me edit this book, as well as Michael Baker for his relentless commitment to the Lord in getting this book typed here in prison, despite all the obstacles.

I thank all the Brothers here in prison with me who have "Fought the Good Fight of Faith", laboring day in and day out to win souls for our Lord and Savior, Jesus Christ.

As well Special Thanks to Chaplain John & Andi Bayer from "Free at Last Prison Ministries", for typing a workable copy and making ready for publishing and distribution, Jimmy Swaggart, Son-Life Broadcasting and those at JSM, to Chaplains and inmates, Al and Jean Dager from Media Spotlight, Alan and Joann Woody from Mission Possible, Ray Hall from the Prison Book Project, Chaplain Mary Ellen Kerr, Bill and Abby Dattilo, and everyone else who has so graciously reached out to those of us in prison.

"GREAT IS YOUR REWARD IN HEAVEN"

Brief Testimony

After a life filled with alcohol and drug abuse, as well as too much other sin to mention, Russell Nestor was eventually led to the Lord Jesus Christ one night in November, 2000. Four months later, though, he was incarcerated and facing a lengthy prison term. The Lord used all of his bad choices and the consequential legal troubles to begin to break him.

After losing at trial, Russell was sentenced to thirty-five years. He spent his first five years in a maximum security federal penitentiary in Coleman, Florida. He was then transferred to a medium security prison in Yazoo City, Mississippi, where he is currently being held.

It was through Son-Life Radio being broadcast in Mississippi that Russell began to hear and understand The Message of The Cross, which has since revolutionized his walk and service to the Lord.

I Corinthians 1:18 "For the Preaching of the Cross is to them who perish foolishness; but unto us which are saved it is the Power of God."

Dedication

This book is dedicated to the two men in my life whom the Lord has used to show me and teach me what it truly means to love and sacrifice yourself for someone else: My Father, John Nestor, and my dear friend, Brother Jeremiah (Jerry) Maney.

Your efforts were not in vain.

Table of Contents

Section II: Other People

Section III: Help for Your Ministry

Section 1: YOU

The Great End Time Harvest Mission Field

"Part of the Army of the Lord"

Introduction

Before reading this book, you need to stop and ask yourself "What is the purpose of my being in prison?" Do you wish to simply serve your time and get out, or, perhaps, even die there, if you have a life sentence or death sentence? Or, despite the mess you're in, is it that God is giving you the opportunity to serve Him?

This book was written for incarcerated men and women who desire to use their time to serve the Lord to the best of their abilities despite their circumstances. If you only wish to get out of prison, this book is not for you. However, if you sincerely desire to allow the Lord to clean you up and use you, then following the teachings of this book will help you reach this goal.

Understand this: only two things will matter the day you die.

1) Whether you know Christ as your personal Savior.

2) Whether you dedicated your life to His service here on earth. Furthermore, the Holy Spirit absolutely must initiate and direct this service, because God always rejects works initiated by our flesh.

In this book are practical, Biblical principles to show you how to grow in Grace yourself, while winning souls for Christ, and making a difference in the lives of those around you.

The Lord wants to share this great labor of love with those who will separate themselves to this calling. There are great rewards for those who will respond to this call and step-out in faith:

A) You will enjoy a closer communion with the Lord, which is reserved for those who trust and obey.

B) You will experience the fulfillment found only in His perfect will.

C) You will receive the rewards God intends for you to have as you stand before the Judgment Seat of Christ.

How disappointing it would be to have nothing to give back to Jesus when you see Him face to face after all He has given to us.

This service to the Lord will require great sacrifices. Servitude or ministry is about the will of the Father. Humility and self-sacrifice are the requirements.

I congratulate you for your willingness to have a ministry while you are locked-up. Few desire to do so, but the prisons are full of men who are lost and headed for Hell, unless the Gospel of Jesus Christ and Him Crucified is preached and taught to them, from the inside.

I sincerely wish you the best, and I believe as you are committed to ministry behind bars the Lord will be working with you to guide your every step.

Please contact Chaplain John at **Free at Last Prison Ministries, P.O. Box 84051, Baton Rouge, Louisiana 70884,** and tell us how your ministry is coming along. May the Lord Bless You Abundantly.

Brother Russell

"Preach the CROSS, to the LOST at any COST"

The Reason This Book Needed To Be Written

A prisoner myself, I see daily hundreds of men who do not know Jesus Christ as their Savior and Lord. Think about that! God has situated us where we have access to and contact with men (women in women's prison) who have already experienced pain and suffering firsthand by being arrested and isolated from society. Done correctly, you can impact these people's lives and forever change them. Since you already have Salvation yourself (I assume) then your focus needs to be the Lord's work, leading men to Jesus. What He did on the Cross is the only answer to their problems in life. It is really that simple. We will work on "how" together, but as long as you are willing, God can and will make a way for you.

Matthew 7:7-12,"Ask, and it shall be given you; seek, and you shall find; knock, and it shall be opened unto you: For every one who asks receives; and he who seeks finds; and to him who knocks it shall be opened. Or what man is there of you, whom if his son ask bread, will he give him a stone? Or if he asks a fish, will he give him a serpent? If you then, being evil, know how to give good gifts unto your children, how much more shall your Father which is in Heaven give good things to them who ask Him? Therefore all things whatsoever you would that men should do to you, do you even so to them.."

Whether or not you approve of the prison system, prisons are being built and filled with amazing speed. We see a steady decline of help from the prison authorities in leading inmates to the only possible source for true help, the Lord Jesus Christ. So the lead needs to be taken by those prisoners who are Christians. There may not be staff members who serve the Lord where you are, but regardless of circumstances, you, as a Believer, have the duty to minister to those around you. And who better? Do you think it is the next man's job?! Of course not. Do you not value your salvation? Chances are someone witnessed to you **(see Romans 10:13-15)** through words and /or deeds. So the Love that He has given us compels us. Jesus came preaching the Kingdom of God: Love, Healing, and Forgiveness.

He continues His Ministry through us, "The Body of Christ." This book will guide you down the path, and help you avoid the mistakes that I have made.

Let me assure you: if you are willing, God will use you. You can be a great blessing to those around you, but you must be willing to allow the Holy Spirit to clean you up and empower you for service. Some things will have to go; "SELF" first! Great men of God are not born great, but will become great by Faith: Faith in what He has done, and what He can and will do if they are willing to serve God, His way.

What I have seen occur in prison, despite the evil environment and lukewarm "Christians", is when one man takes a stand for the Truth and does service for the Lord, others will soon follow, albeit a small group at first. That is what happened here at this prison. Unfortunately I lacked the benefits of an instructional manual geared towards this specific situation. Not to take away from the authority or practicality of God's Word, or the complete personal reliance upon the Holy Spirit, but I believe the Spirit will use our experiences in this book to help you prevent avoidable mistakes and maximize the effectiveness in your prison ministry. I have experienced many inmates who have a zeal for God and His people, but who do not know where to begin or how to be effective. To avoid the discouragement of trial and error I present these proven guidelines based on the Word of God.

Count the Cost

Before you proceed, you need to stop and consider the cost of being a disciple of Jesus Christ; setting out to witness and be a minister in prison; and then evaluate the depth and quality of your desire. The desire must be pure, from a heart devoted to the Glory of God, not a heart seeking self-promotion or praises from men. Read what Jesus said in **Luke 14:27-33** about counting the cost.

If you are unprepared for the great sacrifices that are required of servants of Jesus, you will be like that man who intended to build a tower, but was unable to finish it after he had laid the foundation. You have to want this! You cannot be successful in this endeavor if you are simply looking for something "good" to do. However, this passionate desire, like everything that is truly good, must originate from the heart of God, not from us (see **Romans 7:18.**) When our hearts are on one accord with the heart of God, His Spirit wills and works in us and carries us through the struggles we will face in ministry.

HEAR ME VERY CAREFULLY: you cannot serve God with an ulterior motive! You cannot barter your freedom or anything else for your service. You have to be willing to serve Him whether or not you ever get out of prison. God requires **UNCONDITIONAL SURRENDER**.

So ask yourself: "What is my goal, and why?" If your goal is to be used of God, which is your "reasonable service," then you are on the right track. This work has a price, particularly in the area of "Self."

Here is what you can expect: Opposition from within the Church and outside the Church:

Within: Unfortunately, most of your opposition will come from within the "church." Those who serve the flesh will always persecute those who serve in the Spirit by Faith in the finished work of Jesus.

Without: This opposition is more understandable and expected. The world, the flesh and the Devil hate righteousness.

Rejection: (Again, primarily from within the "church") Anyone whose comfort-zone or "golden calf" is threatened by the Message of the Cross, the true Gospel, will react defensively and aggressively. In order to remain humble, and not be drawn into a fight, you have to remember that the rejection is of Jesus Christ and what He did at Calvary and not of you personally. (See chapter on HUMILITY.)

God to take everything away: In order to minister effectively, God must be your every-thing. To the extent God allows, the enemy will attack you in order to discourage your efforts. Like in the case of Job, he will take everything that he can, and especially your joy. God, in turn, will strip from your grasp anything that comes between you and Him for His Glory and your benefit. The process is called, "purging."

Sacrifice: Expect to lose personal time, focus, privacy, rigid schedules, friends, property (books, clothes, Bibles, etc.), dignity, and pride as you draw closer to Him.

Being refined: Expect the Lord to show you all of your flaws and the ugliness of your character. As you draw "closer" to Him, you will see just how unlike Him you really are.

Still want to do this? If the answer is **"no"**, then do not begin your ministry yet. Ministry is a calling, a gift from the Spirit! Under no circumstances do you proceed because you feel obligated to do so. If you feel called but unprepared, do not jump the gun. The Lord will instruct and empower you in His time. If the answer is **"Yes"**, then the process has already begun! Praise the Lord.

Of course, there are pleasant things to expect, as well:

A closer relationship with the Father will be had. God is only pleased with our Faith in Jesus, which is strengthened by the trials of life and ministry.

Favor with God and men.

Divine Providence: God will supernaturally provide for all or your needs, both personal and for His Ministry.

Abundant Blessing: Trust and obedience bring spiritual, emotional, mental, physical, and financial benefits, not only to us, but to those around us.

If counting the cost has exposed doubt or discouragement, remember that God is with you and the work is His to perform. God is able to do anything and use anyone. God is not interested in your ability; He is looking for your <u>avail</u>-ability! God will give you all you need, including wisdom, materials, and courage. He wants your willingness and trust.

First Things First: the RIGHT MESSAGE

The most important part of your ministry is the foundational Message. It is not about feeding people or trying to change their behavior, or even keeping them out of Hell. It is about the Gospel – the "Good News", that undeserving sinners like we are can know God, and have a relationship with Him, which is what God desires. God loves us. He HATES Sin. Our sin interferes with the relationship we were created to have with Him. There is only one way for this broken relationship to be fixed: the Cross!

This is the foundational Message of all scripture and of any ministry that will make any eternal difference. The only way to be reconciled with God is through faith in Jesus Christ and His completed work which took place on the Cross at Calvary. If you preach or teach any other solution or answer for anything, you are misleading, deceiving, and wasting time. Trusting in Jesus and what He has done, and God's acceptance of Jesus' Offering /Sacrifice, is the only answer, the only solution. Salvation, spiritual growth (sanctification), prayer requests, favor from God, the filling/baptism/power of the Holy Spirit, and everything good we get from God, was purchased by Jesus in His perfect life and His death on the Cross. With most of the modern "church" teaching that overcoming sin in our lives comes by our own efforts, such as "trying harder", "more Bible study", "fasting", etc., it is imperative that you understand these things will NEVER give you victory over sin, the world or the Devil. God does not give victory to us through fleshly efforts, but only to Christ, and what He accomplished for us at Calvary. We receive Jesus' victory over sin by Grace through Faith (belief and trust) in Jesus and what He did on the Cross at Calvary and not through our own efforts or good works. It is all because of what Jesus did for us.

If this is unfamiliar, do yourself a favor and get yourself an "EXPOSITOR'S STUDY BIBLE" from Jimmy Swaggart Ministries (JSM). If you cannot afford the complete Bible, the ministry will send you a cost free copy of the New Testament Bible, to all inmates and service members at no charge, simply by writing and asking for one. Take advantage of this! Do not let anything get in the way of you obtaining the best Study Bible available today. Whether or not you know Brother Swaggart's name, you must realize that the power is in the Message, not in the messenger. JSM preaches the Message of the Cross, and the success of your ministry will depend upon your understanding of this Message. Your life will be transformed as you understand and apply the Message, not only in terms of Salvation, but for everything for which you come to God. All of our blessings come through the Cross of Christ (what He accomplished by His Sacrifice). Our access to even speak with God is because and through our faith in that Sacrifice.

God is only pleased by properly-placed faith. The ministry is about Jesus, not you or the quality/quantity of your performance. A belief based on works and or keeping laws is called "religion." God honors our efforts only if we do things His way, for His reasons.

The real driving force behind any effective ministry is the Holy Spirit. He is called the Spirit of God because He is God. The Holy Spirit comes into our hearts when we exhibit faith in the Cross. God pours out His Grace and Favor upon us when (and only when) we are in Christ, by faith. Not faith in Jesus *"and"* our works. God is not pleased with our good works. Ever! He is pleased (and responsive to) our faith; the good works that follow are the works of God in us. This should remove our pride and Self-satisfaction. The Holy Spirit is not a tool to use. He is God. We need Him to rule, direct, and empower us. Anything you do without His explicit instruction (however good the work may seem, even soul winning or prayer meetings) is a work of the flesh, and is rejected by God. You must have the power of God in the Holy Spirit to minister, or you just waste your time and effort. Without Him you will fail every time. God will oppose any works you perform outside of being obedient by faith. Everything the Father does in our lives and ministries is through His Holy Spirit. This Victory (all His works are Victorious) is always based on Jesus' finished work on the Cross, and it honors Him. The Father gives Christ Victory, and never us, which is why we can only have Victory in Him, in Christ. Listen to me carefully: the only way the Spirit of God can work for us is if our trust is completely in Jesus' sacrifice *alone,* not in His sacrifice and our good behavior. This should bring you relief and rest. If this is new to you, reread it. This "Good-News" is just that simple, and it is exclusive. There is no other way. Jesus said in:

John 14:6,"No man comes to the Father but by Me."
This statement is not limited to salvation, but includes all for which we go to God.

God tells us in: *Isaiah 55:8-9,"My thoughts are not your thoughts, neither are your ways My ways, saith the Lord. Vs. 9, "For as the heavens are higher than the earth, so are My ways higher than your ways, and My thoughts higher than your thoughts. "*

God sees the entire picture of what is going on: **WE DO NOT**. You need the guidance of the Holy Spirit continuously, everyday.

Just imagine: A good friend of yours hires you on at his very successful company as one of his representatives. You, not knowing much about the business, would need his training and instruction in all you do as an employee. However, you take it upon yourself to look around this company and see what you think needs to be changed and improved. Instead of learning from your very successful friend, you decide to show him, despite your lack of experience, how much you can improve his company. How ridiculous!, yet familiar. How often this happens when God brings us into His business of saving souls, bringing people into right relationship with Him.

You need to understand: This ministry is God's business. He has given us the honor and privilege to participate, expecting that we will be trained, guided, and empowered by Him. We do not want to discredit or bring shame to the ministry, which is all that can happen, if we depend on *"SELF"*. We are never to lean-upon or look-to our own understanding, self will, self confidence, intellect, plans. This always leads to self-reliance, self-esteem, and self-indulgence, also known as: **The lust of the flesh, the lust of the eyes, and the pride of life**. You must never make plans and ask God to bless them! You seek Him first and His will for any endeavor (in your life and ministry). The results will always be successful and you will be blessed with a greater ministry. Remember, you are called to rest (Read **Matt. 11:28-30)**, the work is the Lord's. God says, in **Zechariah 4:6, "Not by might, nor by power, but by My Spirit, saith the Lord of hosts."**

Proverbs 3:5-6, "Trust in the Lord with all your heart; and lean not unto your own understanding. In all of your ways acknowledge Him, and He shall direct your path."

How, then do we receive this guidance and power? Jesus will baptize us with His Holy Spirit. The Baptism of the Holy Spirit is a full Spirit possession. This is a must for you if you wish to be of any use to the Master and His Ministry. The Baptism of the Holy Spirit with the evidence of speaking with other tongues is the "power" God promised in *Acts 1:8,"But you shall receive power after that the Holy Spirit is come upon you and you shall be witnesses unto me both in Jerusalem, and Judea, and in Samaria, and unto the uttermost part of the Earth."* THIS IS CRITICAL!!! DO NOT OVERLOOK THIS!!! There is no other acceptable way to serve Him. Without the Baptism of the Holy Spirit you are like a lamp without electricity, a ship without a sail, a gun without bullets. You are useless to the ministry so long as you rely on yourself. You will do more damage than good. It is a wonderful gift that God wants to give to you.

Luke 11:13,"If you then, being evil, know how to give good gifts unto your children: how much more shall your Heavenly Father give the Holy Spirit to them who ask Him?"

If you want this precious gift, but are unsure how to obtain it, simply ask the Lord for it and receive it by faith. You can, as well, ask someone who has been Baptized with the Spirit to pray with you, anoint you with oil, lay hands on you, etc.. Keep in mind, Jesus is the Baptizer, not the person praying for you. If you cannot find someone who has been Baptized with the Holy Spirit, write to Chaplain John at "Free at Last Prison Ministries", and he will send you a free copy of "HOW to be BAPTIZED with the HOLY SPIRT." Make no mistake, *you do need this powerful gift.*

To recap: Ministry depends upon your being rooted in the understanding of the Message of the Cross, being Baptized by the Holy Spirit, and being led by the Holy Spirit in all you do. Be wise and follow God's lead. Put first things first!

Your Flesh

On Judgment Day, the only actions for which you will be called to give an account are yours. Not to say that you are not your Brother's keeper, but he must give account for himself, and you for yourself. You need to examine yourself by God's standards and do some real housecleaning. You are the temple of the Holy Spirit, and whatever is not of Him must go. We must decrease as He increases. God cannot fill us to the extent that He wants with His Holy Spirit when we are full of ourselves (i.e.—pride, lust, bitterness, un-forgiveness, etc.), so some changes need to be made if we wish to minister most effectively. The death to "Self", to which Jesus calls us, is likened to a crucifixion, slow and painful. The Lord tells us *in:*

LUKE 9:23, *"If any man will come after me, let him deny himself, and take up his cross daily, and follow me."*

Your flesh will fight the changes each step of the way. Your flesh despises leaving its comfort zone, and fears the unfamiliar.

God tells us: in *I John 2:15-17, "Love not the world, neither the things that are in the world. If any man love the world, the love of the Father is not in him. For all that is in the world, the lust of the flesh, and the lust of the eyes, and the pride of life, is not of the Father, but is of the world. And the world passes away, and the lust thereof: but he who does the Will of God abides forever."*

Your Pride

The area that you need to first examine is that of pride. There is no place for pride in the life of a Believer, and that needs to be emphasized even more for someone in ministry. Pride is about "SELF." It is so deceptive because it comes in so many different forms. It is your flesh lying to you, and you believing it. And pride will greatly hinder your testimony and ministry, if not ruin them both. Pride tells a man that he does not have to listen to others when they tell him something. Pride puffs up. When pride is in your life, your growth and service to the Lord are brought to a screeching halt. Why? Because you have chosen your pride over God's ways; you are putting *"SELF"* first and not God. You must ask yourself many questions in this area, such as, "Do I see pride in myself?" If the answer is "No", then go back and ask the question again! No one is exempt from its clutches, not even the most dedicated servant of the Lord. It is an issue we will cover over and over in this book because in all you do, your pride will try to take over when it can. You must ask yourself also, "Why am I in the ministry? Is it to serve myself—my pride — am I really called?, or am I a surrendered servant of the Lord?" As well, you must come to terms with whether or not you are WILLING to give up your pride — as best as you can — and allow the Holy Spirit to keep that **"Old Man"** of yours crucified with Christ. You cannot have both your pride and a successful ministry. One or the other will prevail. Immediately after the current decision, discomfort will follow, but as you grow in grace, humility will become second nature.

Pride is the ugliest thing of which I know. It is the most far-reaching sin in the Bible, and so dreadful that it is the sin that cost Lucifer his position and relationship with God, and turned him into the being we now know as Satan. The Bible tells us that pride comes before a fall. This example should be an alarming wake-up call for all of us. Pay close attention to the effects of pride as you go through the topics in this book. The issue of pride is so extremely important both to recognize and prevent, that we will review it again and again. If you wish to grow in grace, your pride must be slain. Here is what God has said to us in,

Matthew, 23:12, "And whosoever shall exalt himself shall be abased; and he that shall humble himself shall be exalted."

"Exalt himself", means to be lifted up in pride. If you are serious about ministry in prison or elsewhere, you need to carefully examine your motivation, your intentions, thoughts and desires, and turn them over to the Lord, which is a demonstration of faith in Him, whereas pride is a demonstration and reliance on "Self." God's power, which the Holy Spirit is to us, was made available to us by Jesus' finished work on the Cross. Pride is therefore defeated when we seek to access this power by trusting fully in Jesus' Sacrifice, not in what we have done, are doing, or will do. You must understand: In pride (self-reliance/self dependence) we not only lose God's power, but we set Him completely against us and our efforts. Pride is idolatry: "Self" before God; sin before God; or things before God. God does not bless or put His approval on any of man's self helps, but in fact He defeats any effort or plan outside of His own. *I Peter 5:5, "God resists the proud and gives grace to the humble."*

So what is the answer to this entire pride problem? The Cross of Jesus Christ! Humility is a Fruit of the Holy Spirit, an evidence of properly placed faith.

Humility

In God's Word pride and humility stand in opposition to each other. Pride is always shown in a negative light, humility in a positive light. From the Garden of Eden to now, pride is and always has been the downfall of man. We overcome pride the same way we receive humility, by grace through faith in Jesus Christ and His Sacrifice at Calvary. If I were to ask you what you did at the Cross of Calvary, and you were honest with yourself, you would have to say "NOTHING". Clearly, Jesus Christ did it all:

Romans 5:8, "While we were yet sinners, Christ died for us."

This alone should be a very humbling and sobering thought. Understanding that He has paid it all, and we have paid nothing, what right do we have to become "puffed-up" about anything? Remember: this is not your ministry. It belongs to God. You are only entrusted with it. The moment "Self" enters into the ministry you have poisoned and sabotaged it. The very word "ministry" means "service"; not the service of "Self", but of the Lord.

I cannot express enough to you the importance of this chapter's subject. The modern church and it's preachers know very little, if anything, about humility. Because humility is a Fruit of the Spirit, its absence in the lives of the church leaders clearly indicates that they are working in the flesh, and not being led by the Holy Spirit. It is a tragedy beyond description. This is why the enemy has been able to infiltrate the church smoothly and easily, filling it with false doctrine and its teachers.

Every man of God must be humbled if he is to be used for service or ministry. You cannot have an effective ministry without the humility. As a young Believer, I fought against being humbled because my flesh resisted at every opportunity. However, I soon began to tire of blaming others, complaining all the time, being humiliated, having to admit that I was wrong when my pride was telling me not to give-in, apologizing to others, having to ask for forgiveness, having to clean up the mess that my pride had caused (offenses, etc), and, overall, feeling like an idiot because I was too proud to humble myself and do the right thing. I learned, at times, while kicking and screaming against the truth, that if you desire to serve God, but refuse to humble yourself, you will be humbled by the Lord, and it is not pleasant!.

Do the right thing: if you are wrong, admit it quickly. If you are not sure of something, do not speak as though you know the answer. If you have offended someone, go to them and apologize immediately. If you think you are better in God's sight than someone else, repent immediately of this absurdity and admit you are not. The longer you wait to humble yourself, the worst it is for you, and the more damage you cause yourself and those with whom you interact! The Bible calls a man who refuses to humble himself, a "fool." Do not be that person. Be wise; obey the Lord and humble yourself before the mighty hand of God that you maybe exalted.

I Peter 5:5-6, "Yes, all of you be subject one to another, and be clothed with humility: for God resists the proud and gives grace to the humble. Humble yourselves therefore under the mighty hand of God, that He may exalt you in due time."

Proverbs 15:33, "The fear of the Lord is the instruction of wisdom; and before honor is humility."

Luke 14:11, "For whosoever exalteth himself shall be abased (this speaks of self-exaltation, which the Lord cannot tolerate) , and he who humbles himself shall be exalted (humility, which can only come by a proper understanding of the Cross, is the requirement for advancement by the Lord).

31

In the beginning, humility hurts. The flesh (Self) dies hard. However, if you keep your faith placed in the Gospel of the Cross, despite the extreme discomfort of dying to "Self", pride will die, and humility will grow with the other fruit of the Spirit. Because humility is such an important issue in your walk and service, you need to safeguard it on a moment by moment basis. A daily general-inspection is not good enough! Pride is so very sneaky. Pride, left un-checked, will make short work of your new-found humility, which is so fragile. By now, you must see how pride and humility are so intertwined that they must be handled simultaneously.

Years ago I came-up with a saying I think puts things into perspective: "Humility is the grease that allows the wheels of Christian growth to turn." No Humility, No Growth!

Matt. 25:36,"Naked, and you clothed Me: I was sick, and you visited Me: I was in prison, and you came unto Me."

To Be Crucified With Christ

The term "Crucified with Christ" identifies a mind-set of humility perfectly demonstrated by Jesus. Read the following verses from:

Philippians 2:3-8, "Let nothing be done through strife or vainglory; but in lowliness of mind let each esteem other better than themselves. Look not every man on his own things, but every man also on the things of others. Let this mind be in you, which was also in Christ Jesus: Who, being in the form of God, thought it not robbery to be equal with God: But made Himself of no reputation, and took upon Him the form of a servant, and was made in the likeness of men: And being found in fashion as a man, He humbled Himself, and became obedient unto death, even the death on the Cross."

To be crucified with Christ is a position in God's mind in which He places you into Jesus' actual life and death; therefore in His mind, you have already lived and died. The rest of your mortal existence on earth no longer belongs to you. God says, **"You are bought with a price."** The remainder of your life belongs to God, Who, if you are submissive, as your end of the agreement entails, exercises His rightful possession of what He has bought. So long as His Holy Spirit is empowering and guiding, the Lord will bring Himself glory, and your life will evidence the Fruit of the Spirit. While your spirit also remains in your body, it should be there only to witness the work of God, which is a learning or schooling experience for us, His children.

Problems arise when you are not surrendered completely to His presence and authority. As soon as we take control back from God, we immediately set ourselves up for failure.

Out of the flesh comes no good thing because we are not strong enough to keep the flesh in subjection; only the Spirit of God has the power to overcome sin, and He has given us that power through our faith in Jesus' Sacrifice. From the moment you accept Jesus as your Lord and Savior, in every decision you make you are to consider the glory of God, not the comfort or convenience of your flesh, the enemy of God. That is what it means to be crucified with Christ. It is a slow, agonizing death of your flesh. Paul's driving desire was recorded for us in,

Philippians 3:10, "That I may know Him, and the power of His resurrection, and the fellowship of His sufferings, being made conformable unto His death."

Most people leave off the end of this verse, especially the "prosperity preachers." We are to emulate Jesus, who was obedient unto death, even to death on the Cross. When you are on the cross, Jesus is on the throne; when you are on the throne (taking control of your life) Jesus is on the Cross. His place is always to be on the throne.

Being an Example

People primarily learn lessons in life by being taught general principles verbally and by demonstration. Children learn from the examples set by their parents, as students learn from their teachers. In your ministry it makes no difference what you have to tell people if your life is not an example of your teachings. Jesus calls us to be examples, not only in our words, but also in our lifestyles. You must recognize that it is humanly impossible to set the example and perform the works to which we are called. However, God is not playing games with us; He is not commanding us to do something that is not achievable. Christians are, in fact, called to live miraculous lives that bring Him the glory in all that we do. The Holy Spirit can only use us as an example when our faith is squarely placed in the Cross. Our understanding and the example we set needs to be: "Look what the Lord has done, and what Jesus can do in the life of someone who will trust Him," not, "Look what a good person I am and what I have done." Anytime we divert the glory or credit to ourselves and away from Jesus, we betray Him, sabotage the ministry and we frustrate His grace. In time, as your faith continues to be directed at Calvary, not yourself, you will be used as a greater and greater example of the Power of God in the life of someone who is truly Spirit-Led. As long as you retain the humility of Jesus in your life, and refrain from becoming arrogant or puffed-up, you will be used mightily.

When Paul told Timothy in *I Timothy 4:12, "Be thou an example of the Believers in word, in conversation, in charity, in spirit, in faith, in purity.",* his expectation was not for

Timothy to attempt to accomplish these things through his own efforts or abilities, but to allow himself to be used by the Spirit, which is evident in his further instruction to Timothy in the same letter *I Timothy 6:12, "Fight the good fight of Faith."* Paul knew the key to success as an example is our faith being in Christ's finished work and not in our own.

Everyone hates a hypocrite! Don't be that guy. Firstly, if you are not actually living this life of victory and blessing, you are missing out on the wonderful life God wants for you. Jesus told us that He has come to give you not just life, but to give you an abundant life (plenty, wealth, affluence, etc.) In other words, a spiritual rich and enjoyable life that is exciting. Secondly, people want you to put your money where your mouth is, to "practice what you preach". You have probably heard the old adage, "physician, heal yourself." This is not unfair on their part. How can you expect people to follow an example you have not set? Demonstrate Jesus' Victory over sin in your life because it will paint a picture, and as you have heard, "A picture is worth a thousand words."

Being Real

In prison, the people we are trying to reach see us twenty-four hours a day. We cannot just put on our "holy mask" for church and fake-out the rest of the congregation. This is a good thing. It forces us to make a choice; a life choice. Prisoners especially expect a Christian to live like Christ. God does too. And who wants to be a fake? If the Message of the

Cross is new to you, this may sound strange, but, the only way to be truly REAL is to REST in Him. If you are not convinced of this and still feel that you need to impress God and those around you with your "magnificent works" then read the following over and over until gets into your spirit. See who it is that performs all the work: the Lord Jesus Christ, by His Holy Spirit.

Psalms 23, "The Lord is my Shepherd; I shall not want. He makes Me to lie down in green pastures: He leads Me beside the still waters. He restores My soul, He leads Me in the path of Righteousness for His Name's sake. Yes, though I walk through the valley of the shadow of death, I will fear no evil, for You are with Me, Your rod and staff they comfort Me. You prepare a table for Me in the presence of My enemies: You anoint My head with oil; My cup runs over. Surely goodness and mercy shall follow Me all the days of My life: and I will dwell in the House of the Lord forever."

Matthew 11: 28-30, "Come unto Me all you who labor and are heavy laden, and I will give you rest. Take My yoke upon you and learn of Me, for I am meek and lowly in heart and ye shall find rest unto your souls. For my yoke is easy, and My burden is light."

It is Jesus (through the Holy Spirit) that makes us Christians, not our performance, knowledge, or sincerity. He changes us from the inside out. He transforms our entire world-views and thought processes. When our thought-patterns and desires are conformed to those of the Lord, we are real and open to be read by others. The reason we are then real is that we are doing what we desire and live to do, which is real. The good works are not a "front" to convince people that we are "holy," it is not an act; it is who we really are and want to be. Also, because our hearts and desires have now changed, we continue in appropriate behavior even when other people cannot see us, even when we are alone. Just "rest" and let God do His work in you!!!

To avoid misunderstandings, let me be clear on what rest is not. Rest is not an absence of work; it is rest from self-reliance. It is not that you will not have good works, acts of charity, kind and loving gestures, etc., that follow the Born-Again experience. Because your heart and mind have been regenerated (made new by His Spirit) you do not have to search for good things to do to show yourself to be a good Christian in order to convince others or please Jesus.

II Corinthians 5:17,"Therefore if any man be in Christ, he is a new creature: all things are passed away; behold all things are become new."

Your actions do not please Jesus, the state of your heart does, and the actions will automatically flow because they are the natural outflow of who you are becoming. So to "sum-it-up" it is not your body at rest; your mind and spirit are in a state of peace and rest. This is the rest of which the Bible speaks.

When you are "working" (which stems from "self") instead of "resting" (which is found only in Christ by faith), you will not actually have victory, but will have to pretend that you do. You will have to fake-it because people expect Christians to be like Jesus, and you are not. You will not be real and others will see right through this. You must understand that the more we ourselves do, the less real we are, and people will automatically put us in the "Fake" category. As well as being surrendered and real in your walk and service, you must be wise in all you do. You must ask God for this wisdom which He will freely give.

James 1:5," If any of you lack wisdom (pertains to proper knowledge of the Word of God) let him ask of God, Who gives to all men liberally and upbraideth not; and it shall be given him. "

The Bible says to **"Abstain from all appearance of evil" and to "Let not your good be evil spoken of".** People will twist and turn what you say, and use the good you are doing against your ministry. They will lie about you and assassinate your character. You will not be able to stop them, but you can do your best not to give them unnecessary ammunition. Being real, which requires being surrendered to God's will and allowing the Lord to shine His humility and love through you, will enable you to make progress in the ministry of which God has allowed you to be a part. If you are not real, you are wasting your time.

One of the many valuable lessons I learned at the U.S.P. (United States Penitentiary) is shown in this story: There was a very large population of men from Washington D.C. who were a very tight-knit group that generally kept their distance from others. If you were not from D.C. you were not easily trusted by them. Most of these men came from very difficult and rough backgrounds, so they had seen all the tricks, scams, and cons. They were not looking for more, so befriending someone new was not something they easily did. However, during my time there, the Lord gave me favor with them, which His Words says He will do:

Proverbs 3:4, "So you shall find favor and good understanding in the sight of God and man."

I was accepted and trusted by them, even though I was neither from D.C. nor the skin color they were. I saw that many of these men trusted me more than some of the men from their own area, even some who were Christians. One day, after a situation, two men brought me into a cell and explained to me, "Brother Russell, we trust you because you are real." That was a huge eye-opening experience for me. I began to understand that these men were not expecting perfection from someone who says he is a Christian (because I certainly am not perfect), but they will judge you as to whether or not they believe you are real in your walk. This means that even men who truly know the Lord, but are still holding on to some ways that are of the world, will be perceived as not being real by many. Is this fair that we are judged this way? No, but who said anything about fair? Our concern is effective ministry in prison. The men will not listen to you until they respect you, and they will not respect you unless you are real.

In men we despise weakness and admire strength. As Christians this is to our advantage since we do not have to derive strength from within ourselves. We can draw from the infinite strength of God. The reality is that all men have weaknesses, which most men hide, especially in a prison setting. You do not have to project a "hard" image in order to hide flaws or weaknesses. Your safety, confidence and power come from

God. You receive them freely from God because Jesus purchased them with His own blood. You do not need validation or approval from other inmates, staff, or chaplains. When you have God's approval, you do not need the approval of mere men. When you are validated by God, you cannot be manipulated by your own insecurities. There will be none. Knowing God is well-pleased with you because your faith is properly placed, you will walk with a confidence that no one can deny.

Do not try to be real just to further this ministry; be real because God wants you to have real victory, the real joy, the real peace, the real power, and the real blessings that a real relationship will bring. Of course, we know that this is made possibly only by grace through faith in what Jesus Christ did at the Cross. Be real, and wise in all you do.

Your Word

One thing I have seen cause problem after problem in prison is men not keeping their word to each other. Prison-life demands that you interact with others, and people depend on your keeping of your word. Problems arise when someone does not honor his word, and the other person (s) involved feels as though he has been deceived and/or exploited. Arguments and/or violence often result. A man who fails to keep his word quickly develops a bad reputation.

In ministry, if you have a problem keeping your word,

you cannot expect to draw people to the Lord through your example. If you are inconsistent or undependable, no one will listen to you or take you seriously. When you say you are going to do something, as the Lord's representative, you had better follow through. Men in prison are looking for someone on whom they can depend. This person on whom they can always depend on should be the Jesus they see inside you, by your actions. When you tell someone that you will pray for them, you had best get it done when you said you would; when you tell him you will meet with him, then you must be there; when you schedule a Bible Study, be sure to show up on time. If you tell someone you will give him a Bible, book to read, Daily Bread, etc. make sure you follow-through (carry a notepad with you, if you cannot remember).

Most of the men around you come from backgrounds of abuse of some type, so they are skeptical and untrusting of others, which is why your word has to be your bond. Otherwise you will be just another one of the many who have failed them. This should never be!

Understand this as well; people, even in prison, will overlook mistakes and things that happen unexpectedly so long as they believe you are real and sincere, and as long as you COMMUNICATE with them when problems arise. Even our most ardent opponents know that we Christians make mistakes and encounter unavoidable circumstances. You will earn and keep the respect of those involved if you do your best to share with them what the situation is, and your word will remain intact.

After those very rare emergency situations one

encounters, or the occasional realization that the commitment you have made is unwise, you must realize that how you handle yourself after breaking the news is of utmost importance. When you tell someone you will meet with them on Monday, but soon after you remember that you have a previous commitment (or whatever the case), you must make every effort you can to accommodate the other person by meeting him whenever he is available. If the confusion/problem/cancellation is on your end, you need to go to whatever length to show the individual you are serious about keeping your word/agreement/meeting with him.

In prison, Christians are already perceived by non-believers to be weak, fake, hiding behind the Bible, etc. Do not contribute to this misperception by failing to keep your word. What you do, or do-not do, does not only reflect upon Jesus and the Gospel of Grace, it affects every other Christian on the compound. Remember, you must set the example at all times. Never mind how others handle situations; you need to always do your best to keep your word, and by doing so, maintain your testimony.

KEEP YOUR WORD NO MATTER WHAT!

Honesty in all Things, but being Wise in what you Share

One would assume that the practice of honesty is a given in the lives of Brothers; unfortunately, all too often we see the very opposite taking place in the dealings of those who call themselves Christians. Dishonest men forfeit the fulfilling and blessed life of joy that Jesus offers us, and are unprofitable to God for the ministry. Honesty must begin with one's self. You must seek courage and strength from the Lord in order to face the truth about your flaws and shortcomings. Once you are honest with yourself and the Lord, He is then able to clean you up and heal you so you do not have to hide your wounds or mask your weaknesses. Your wounds will be healed and your weakness will be become His strength. Glory to God.

Being dishonest is not just a behavior problem. Jesus said, *Matthew, 13:14, "For out of the abundance of the heart the mouth speaks"*, so this weakness of character runs deeply to the central core of whom one is as a person. You cannot fix yourself; the Holy Spirit will fix you as a result of your willingness, surrender, and trust in the victory that Jesus has already won for us at Calvary.

Part of being an example is being honest in all your dealings and conversations, even though you may expose a fault of your own. You are the one who has to set the example of being honest wherever you minister, whether in prison, or not. In prison you live in close proximity to others twenty-four hours a day, seven days a week, so you must be sure that everything you do is done with honesty and integrity. You are not called to be legalistic, trying to keep every "rule and regulation" to "show others how honest you are", but you are called to set the example when it comes to dealing with others, including staff members.

Use wisdom in all you do. Though some things may be

no big deal for everyone else to do, they might be a stain to your testimony to anyone who may not understand, and you need to be wise, and likely, refrain from doing them. If something may be perceived as "being dishonest", even though it is really not, then stay away. The credibility of your testimony has to be what you cherish and guard most carefully, along with your relationship with the Lord.

If someone over pays you --- correct the situation immediately. If, while you are at the commissary, you are undercharged somehow – go to the window immediately and correct the mistake. You must realize, everyone will develop a reputation for himself in prison, a good one or a bad one. As a Believer who represents the Lord Jesus Christ, you should gladly welcome this opportunity and do all you can to ensure your reputation is one that highlights honesty. Inmates and staff alike take notice to how you conduct yourself, and whether you are honest in all you do; honesty will be a boost to your ministry, your testimony, and the favor that God will give you in the opportunity to witness to both of these groups. Your ministry is not limited to inmates only!

As much as honesty needs to be stressed, you have to be wise in what you share with others. The fact that someone is a Christian, and that you have developed a close relationship with him, does not mean that he is not a confidential informant who will betray your trust for a sentence reduction. Be Spirit-led always! Do not trust out of emotion. Prison is very lonely; you will want a confidant. Make it Jesus!

There are precious few especially in the "church", who will not hesitate to "throw you under the bus" if it helps them in some way. Be circumspect (cautious)! DO NOT share any uncharged misconduct from your past for which you could be indicted!!! If you feel the need to talk with someone about your past, then talk to the Lord. If the Holy Spirit is leading you to talk with the authorities about something you have done, be obedient. However, you are neither called to share every sin you have ever committed, nor every thought you have with other Believers. When the Bible says in *James 5:16, "Confess your faults one to another"*, it is not telling you to share your sins with the Body of Christ. It is a different story if you sin against someone; in that case you must confess your fault to them alone. Pray for Godly wisdom before you act.

James 1:5, "If any of you lack wisdom, let him ask of God, Who gives to all men liberally, and up-braideth not: and it shall be given him".

Be especially cautious when dealing or sharing with young Believers and men new to the faith. Like it or not, Baby Christians are usually looking up to you, spiritually, so for them to hear about sins from your past may do more to harm than do them good. Again, use the wisdom that God so freely gives to those who ask Him. Listen to the words of the Lord, found in *Matt. 10:16,"Behold, I send you forth as sheep in the midst of wolves; be you therefore wise as serpents, and harmless as doves."*

Communication

Communication is conveying your thoughts or beliefs to

another person. As a Christian, the thoughts and beliefs you are conveying are not your personal opinions, but the absolute truth of God's Holy Word. You should consistently communicate the same message with your actions and behavior that you communicate with your words! Any discrepancies (inconsistencies) between your walk and your talk will render you completely ineffective in your testimony and witness. People dismiss hypocrites. Do not give Satan a "foot in the door" to your life and ministry.

The tongue is the hardest part of self-control, which is a Fruit of the Spirit. If you are completely submitted to the Spirit, He will keep your tongue under His control and use it to glorify God, to heal, help, deliver, set free, and restore the sin sick soul. The Bible says in *Ephesians 4:29, "Let no corrupt communication proceed out of your mouth, but that which is good to the use of edifying, that it may minister grace to the hearers."* As well in the book of *James 3:10-11, "Out of the same mouth proceeds blessing and cursing. My Brethren, these things ought not be so. Does a fountain send forth at the same place sweet water and bitter?"* The Bible tells us these things, but the only way for you to consistently live-out these commands is to properly place your faith in what Jesus has already done for you and me at Calvary.

When you are teaching and preaching the Message of freedom from sin through the Gospel, your life must reflect that you indeed have been freed from sin and bondage. Living a pattern of sin is terrible enough to devastate your effectiveness as an example of Jesus' saving power, but you must also realize that individual acts of sin also tarnish your credibility. Remember: do not take it upon yourself to live a Holy life. Trust

God to manifest and display Jesus' Righteousness in your life through the power of the Holy Spirit as a testimony to His saving and keeping Grace. Do not try to develop your own righteous life; that is the Holy Spirit's responsibility and will.

Understand that the disparity between your walk and your talk will come about because you try to practice what you preach by your own efforts instead of by faith in His ability to perform the work in you that is needed. Rest in Him to perform that which concerns you and your ministry.

Also very important in conveying your message are your interpersonal communication skills. These include, but are not limited to; facial expressions, body language, tone of voice, controlling initial reaction, and manners.

Develop yourself in these areas to be a more effective minister of the Gospel. People are offended by self-righteous, smug facial expressions, as well as improper tone of voice, offensive and defensive body language, bad manners, and uncontrollable reactions to what they are telling you. They will never come to you again once they feel hurt or dismissed by you. Be sure to communicate the love, patience, and compassion of Jesus in every possible way! Make eye contact; do not shake your head, curl your lip in disgust, raise an eyebrow in silent judgment or disapproval, never tap your foot in impatience, etc. Glorify God in every minute detail.

Let the Bible They Read Be You

An old-time preacher once said, **"Out of one hundred people, one will read the Bible, and ninety-nine will read the Christian!!!"** I believe his name was Dwight Moody, and his words still hold true today. Most people will not read the Bible, but they are always reading and watching the Christians. Some may want you to fail, but others desperately want to know if a walk with Christ is real. And what is it that lets them know that you are real? It is the love that you have for those around you. Take the time to read what Paul wrote in,

I Corinthian 13, "Though I speak with the tongues of men and Angels and have not charity (love) I am become as sounding brass, or a tinkling cymbal."

And though I have the Gift of Prophecy, and understand all mysteries, and all knowledge; and though I have all Faith, so that I could remove mountains and have not charity (love), I am nothing.

And though I bestow all my goods to feed the poor, and though I give my body to be burned and have not charity (love), it profits me nothing.

Charity (love) suffers long and is kind, charity envies not, Love vaunts not itself, is not puffed up (is not prideful).

Does not behave itself unseemly, seeks not her own, is not easily provoked, thinks no evil, (takes no account of evil).

Rejoices not in iniquity, but rejoices in Truth.

Bears all things, believes all things, hopes all things (keeps believing for the best), endures all things (puts up with everything).

Love never fails, but whether there be Prophecies, they shall fail; whether there be Tongues, they shall cease; whether there be Knowledge, it shall vanish away.

For we know in part and we Prophesy in part.

But when that which is perfect is come then that which is in part shall be done away.

When I was a child, I spoke as a child, I understood as a child, I thought as a child; but when I became a man, I put away childish things.

For now we see through a glass, darkly, but then face to face (after the resurrection): now I know in part, but then shall I know even as also I am known.

And now abides Faith, Hope, Love, these three (all three will abide forever); but the greatest of these is Love (it is the greatest because Love alone makes us like God).

Read the above over and over until it gets into your Spirit and you really get it!! Remember the Bible is a Love Story: God's Love for us. Love is not found in the religions of the world, except the "love of self". God's Agape Love, when shared with others, is what will attract their attention and touch their hearts.

Love never fails; God says so. If love is not displayed in our lives towards others, and I mean a true, selfless love, which puts others first before ourselves, then those who "read us" will never know the difference between having a relationship with Jesus, and being religious. In fact, if we do not have the love, peace and joy that the Lord provides, shining through our lives, then all we really have is religion. The Bible is about the Lord's un-conditional and never ending Love for us. Let people see that Love in you in all that you do and say in your daily life and ministry.

What is Your Testimony?

Besides your relationship with the Lord, your testimony and your ministry are the most important things for you to protect. As I said before, you must guard them both very carefully. So you must ask yourself, "What is my "testimony?" What do people say about You? How are you perceived by others around you?

Here is what they should not be saying about you: He's a Christian, but he's really grouchy or grumpy or short-tempered at times. No one wants to deal with you if you are offensive to them. Where do these bad traits have their roots? That is right, in that old pride! Do you become defensive easily, also? Guess what that is from? It is that pride again. These traits are testimony-wreckers! As well, here's a partial list of things that will absolutely destroy your testimony as a true Christian and a minister of the Gospel; Profanity, fighting, porn, alcohol, drugs, knives, fornication, insubordination, intemperance, write-ups, gossiping, laziness, "gunning", ogling women, flirting, "snitching", racism, greed, etc.

Here is what they should be saying about you: "He is for real. He is honest. He is joyous. He cares about those around him. He puts others before himself. He does not compromise. He is humble. He is a hard worker. He listens. He Loves the Lord above all else. He is generous. He is a peace maker and problem solver. He keeps his word. He is trustworthy. He helped me to understand Bible questions I had. He prayed for my family. He was there when I needed help. He taught me the Message of the Cross, Jesus Christ and Him Crucified, the one and only true Gospel Message.

There are many things that could be added to the preceding statements. Your actions affect your testimony, one way or the other. If your testimony is stained, your ministry will suffer greatly. People rarely remember the good you do, but be assured, they will always remember and never forget the wrongs you have committed. Do not give in to the temptation of the enemy. Give him no place in your life and testimony. Protect your testimony at all costs, and that cost will be humbling yourself and making sacrifices for others. Remember these simple but profound words: *Sin will take you farther than you wanted to go; Sin will keep you longer than you wanted to stay; and Sin will cost you more than you wanted to pay.*

Now ask yourself this question: If we were to ask those around you what your testimony is, what would they say? It is important what others have to say about us. However, most importantly is, what does God have to say about your walk, talk, and testimony? Does it meet with His approval?

Being Offensive to Others

While offenses come in many different forms, your job, in ministry, is to make sure that you, personally, are not the offensive factor. In other words, there are things that you are going to say to people that are offensive because your Message either convicts them in their heart, or goes against their current belief system. However, even though your Message may be offensive, the way you say it never should be! If your presentation is offensive, it means your pride has infected your side of the conversation. No one wants to listen to a prideful, offensive person, no matter how "correct" they may be. Remember, our aim is not to be 'right" in all we say to others; it is to share the Truth with them in Love. We need to be effective, not shoving down their throats how "right we are". The Word of God is offensive enough to sinful flesh, we do not need to add our own offense to it.

When we are offensive to others we "open the door" for them to dismiss the Message (wrongly) while dismissing the messenger. Their flesh does not need any further excuse to continue running from God. When you share with others the Message of the Cross, which is the only Gospel (Good News) you need to be sharing and teaching, there will be an offense. You be sure to get yourself out of the way, and be loving and humble, which will soften the blow. If your ministry is about "looking right" then you may as well throw in the towel until you humble yourself.

You have to understand, while preaching truth and correct doctrine are essential, only one in a million is won to Jesus by logic and intellect. Knowing that God knows you have your facts straight has to be enough validation for you. Ministers of the Gospel are not to seek approval of men, but of God. People are attracted to love and compassion, not to lectures or facts which contradict their current beliefs.

When you interact with others, *listen to them* as they speak. Be sure you make eye contact so they understand that you are listening. When people are sharing with you, make sure your attention is on them, not on the things around you. Remember, you are there to minister to them and that means showing them concern, courtesy, respect, and attentiveness while you spend time with them. Do not ruin a good opportunity to witness or minister to someone because you are offensive somehow. Hypocrisy, complaining, talking over someone, interrupting, being argumentative, appearing close-minded, etc., will sabotage your ministry. If you are in the fight to win souls for Christ, and make disciples of them, then humble yourself, and stop being offensive.

Being Defensive

While we are not to offend others, they definitely will offend us. We are called to do as the Lord said in *Matthew 5:44,"But I say unto you, Love your enemies, bless them who curse you, do good to them who hate you, and pray for those who despitefully use you, and persecute you."*

As you are beginning to realize, like most sin, defensiveness, has its roots in pride. When you become defensive, the reason is normally that you feel that your opinion was not valued and accepted immediately. You are upset because you feel rejected, not because the Gospel has been rejected. This stems from wrong thinking that you are right, and the other individual is wrong. In reality, God is right, and we are all wrong. Understand this: God is glorified whether the Gospel you have presented is rejected or accepted, whether they bless you or curse you. If you are insulted, it is not on God's behalf, because He has already been glorified; it is because of your pride, thinking to yourself that because you are such an awesome witness or expert on the subject matter that the person should automatically accept what you had to say. Things did not go the way you thought they should have. The Apostle James wrote, by inspiration of the Holy Spirit *in James 1:20,"For the wrath of man worketh not the righteousness of God."* As well, in *Proverbs13:10,"Only by pride cometh contention…"*. We are commanded to praise God, rejoice, be exceedingly glad, and even to "Leap for Joy", *Luke 6:23,"Rejoice ye in that day, and leap for joy; for behold, your reward is great in*

Heaven.... " when, because of your Message and beliefs (lifestyle), you are mistreated. Most Christians, being underprepared for the ministry are shocked and pull back/retreat when this occurs, but, in fact, this is an excellent sign, and one you should embrace whole heartedly. We are not friends with the world, the flesh, or the devil; this is a war. If the world embraces you, they do not consider you an enemy, so God probably does. You have to learn to cherish the resistance in order to be effective. After all, is this not the goal of your ministry?

A dear Brother once said to me, "Brother Russell, a dead man can't be offended." What did he mean by that statement? He meant, we as Christians, are to die with Christ on the Cross. We do this by faith in what He did for us. We are then raised to Life with Him. That "Old Man" of ours, which is where all that pride resides, is supposed to stay dead --- crucified--- and we are to walk in newness of life, which includes humility. When the offenses come, which they will, the Love of Jesus continues to deal with others through us, so long as the pride and defensiveness remain dead, crucified. Look past the offenses and see the need. Keep your eyes on the prize of the high calling of God in Christ Jesus. *Philippians 3:14, "I press towards the mark for the prize of the high calling of God (Christ-likeness) in Christ Jesus.* "

Once you turn defensive, you become offensive, which is an ugly sight, especially in a Believer. Defensive behavior has no place in ministry. No matter what people say or do, do not be rattled. Your job is not to defend God, His Word, or even your ministry. Verbal wrestling does nothing but add fuel to the other person's folly. By engaging in debate or argument you will give your opponent the very false impression that his opinion is relevant; in light of the fact that the Word of the Lord is being presented, there is no argument or debate. D.L.Moody stated, *"The Bible is like a lion; you don't have to defend it, just let it go!"* Remain humble. Treat offensive people kindly, no matter what. Continue to respect the offenders as people, and watch the Holy Spirit work in the situation. Remember, we are not respectful to others because they are respectful people or respectable (because much of the time they are not). We are respectful because we are called to be respectful as ministers of the Gospel and Ambassadors for the Kingdom of Heaven.

It was explained to me as a young Christian that if people see a wise man and a fool arguing in the distance, it is very difficult to distinguish which is the fool. If you are doing the right thing, you do not have to worry about defending your position. When you stand-up for the truth and preach and teach the Message of the Cross, people are going to try to point out what they claim will be your flaws. Do not cast your pearls before swine. Such people are not seeking the truth, so do not witness to them verbally, nor be drawn into spiritual/religious discussions, but continue to witness by demonstrating the love of Jesus in your actions and attitude (lifestyle). The demonstration of true love towards others cannot be easily denied in their hearts, especially after they have been offensive to you. This is why you do not become upset; it is about the Gospel, not your feelings. You will lose the opportunity to witness by becoming defensive. Continue to be kind and gentle, and pray for them.

Do Not Compromise!

In order to not compromise, you must be bold --- supernaturally bold. Look anywhere in the New Testament and you will find displays of this boldness in the uncompromising witness of those Believers acting in the power of the Holy Spirit. This boldness is not given for any old reason; it is given to equip us for ministry, along with the other gifts of the Spirit.

Always remember: this is a war. Satan, our enemy, is trying to make us ineffective. He is very crafty and slick. He will come at us in many ways; he will try to get us to compromise through bullying us, coercion (fear), seduction, greed, flattery, lust, etc., playing on our insecurities, and through our pride. And when Satan cannot effectively attack us directly, he will attack the people we love and the things we cherish. Remember what I said about counting the cost?

In order to avoid compromise with Satan, which is defeat and failure, God and His Righteousness have to be our everything. The Apostle Paul counted everything else as "dung" (refuse, waste, trash) outside of his relationship with the Lord. And so must you! Anything that you really value outside of your relationship with the Lord is a potential hostage waiting to be used against you by Satan.

The enemy will tempt you to compromise in areas of your character, doctrines that are not of God, associations with those who do compromise, indulging in sin, watering down your

Message, with other beliefs (and their gods! Which is always the case), and every other area that he can. When Satan knows that you have begun to compromise (retreat), it will become that much easier for him to convince you to do so again and again.

You may view a compromise on your part as a moment of weakness, but others will see it as hypocrisy. Few leaders today refuse to compromise on matters of importance. Never be that guy! Most "church leaders" do not seek first the Kingdom of God and His Righteousness, but yearn for approval of men and earthly rewards, pleasures, and comforts. Satan's wages are very attractive to the flesh, but the curse of God is the sure result. ***Proverbs 20:17,"Bread of deceit is sweet to man; but afterwards his mouth shall be filled with gravel."***

When it comes to the things of God, you must stand firm. You can compromise with others on incidentals and things that do not relate to the truth and your obedience to God's Word, but on those matters you cannot budge, ever. Remember, people are always watching and listening to see what is real. Many desire and hope to see real leaders make righteous decisions and stick with them.

Particularly in prison, Satan will use various avenues of approach, such as the following:

COMMUNION: Participating in the Lord's Supper is a grave responsibility and privilege, and we are commanded not to partake in it unworthily by not having our faith exclusively in Christ and His Sacrifice for cleansing from sin. Those who do so eat and drink damnation unto themselves. Paul's warning in

I Corin. 11:23-30,"For I have received of the Lord that which also I delivered unto you, That the Lord Jesus the same night in which He was betrayed took bread: Vs 24,"And when He had given thanks, He broke it, and said, Take, eat: this is My Body, which is broken for you: this do in remembrance of Me: vs. 25,"After the same manner also He took the cup, when He had supped, saying, This cup is the New Testament in My Blood: this do you, as oft as you drink it, in remembrance of Me. Vs.26,"For as often as you eat this bread, and drink this cup you do show the Lord's death till He come. vs.27,"Wherefore whosoever shall eat this bread, and drink this cup of the Lord, unworthily, shall be guilty of the Body and Blood of the Lord.vs.28,"But let a man examine himself, and so let him eat of that bread, and drink of that cup. vs.29,"For he who eats and drinks unworthily, eats and drinks damnation to himself, not discerning the Lord's Body." vs. 30,"For this cause many are weakly and sickly among you, and many sleep."

This scripture instructs us to warn unbelievers and disfellowship with those who walk disorderly. If no one is standing before the congregation and warning them of the detrimental effects (possibly even early death!) of wrongful participation, do not participate. If, like in most prison "protestant" services, many inmates, who openly profess to be members of other faiths are enjoining, you must refrain from participation. Do not put your stamp of approval on something that is being abused by those who know better, and is misleading to those who do not!

TIME SLOTS: Do not compromise by calling yourself someone from another faith simply to get a time slot at the chapel. Furthermore, do not soften your Message in order to keep a time slot (or your opportunities to speak, teach, and pray before the congregation or assembly); the slot and opportunities may be threatened when you begin to step on the religious people's toes by setting people free from their bondages of religion and sin, which are one and the same.

ACCESS to MATERIALS: Compromising the faith to simply have access to materials in the chapel is foolish. God will provide all of your needs according to His riches in Glory by Christ Jesus.

PRAYING in JESUS' NAME: Do not compromise with a generic prayer to "God", that you know will be interpreted by hearers as referring to another god, such as Allah, Buddha, etc. If you cannot pray in Jesus name, reject the chance to pray publicly.

NOT BEING ALLOWED TO MEET: in your cells, library, the yard, etc. specifically for Bible Study: Use wisdom but do not compromise. Keep assembling and learning. Study together so you are not influenced by various false doctrines, nor fall to any private interpretation of your own. Christians need each other to grow properly.

CALLING YOU DIVISIVE: Jesus came to bring a sword, and narrow is the way. Most people will never serve God, so disregard their opinions. While it is not our goal to be divisive, the Gospel is, without question. Do not fall into the trap of "coming together" for the sake of "unity". The only unity we seek is unity of the Spirit and Truth. We seek unity with God, not men. God will unite in Spirit those who are for Him. We do not seek unity with false teachers, preachers, or brethren. We will be divided as people; what communion has light with darkness? Just remember: while separating ourselves from the world, we must speak the truth in love always.

PARTICIPATING in OTHER FAITH's SERVICES: Do not do this, ever! We do not worship false gods, or participate in the worship of false gods. Do not speak; do not sing; do not play instruments; do not hand-out literature; do not lend them financial aid; do not invite people to them, etc. Do not do anything that can be perceived as your supporting their service. As a chapel worker, you may carry-out your job, whether that may be setting up chairs, sound equipment, musical instruments, etc. However, do nothing to give the impression that you condone or promote false doctrine or worship false gods! While the invitation to one of these services may give you the opportunity to share the Gospel with someone and allow you to bring them to your service, do not participate in their rituals, pray to their god, or make it a habit of going to their service.

The word of God says in *Exodus 34:14,"For you shall worship no other god: for the Lord, whose name is Jealous, is a jealous God."*

Again Satan's primary avenue of approach will be the "church". Influential "religious" inmates, as well as many prison chaplains, will try to sway you away from your firm stance in the Gospel to join forces with them in preaching and teaching anything and everything except about sin and its only solution: Jesus Christ and Him Crucified, the Message of the Cross. Multi-faith programs, psychology, 12 step programs, Purpose Driven courses, and all else that promotes unity (ecumenism) are not God's agenda. All of our problems stem from sin; the only solution is the Cross; and God's agenda is a close, personal relationship with Him. We must never compromise or deviate from this Message. Be the example ---do not compromise.

Self Examination

One of the toughest things for a man to do is to analyze himself honestly. Our flesh will fight us continually during this process and tell us that there is no need to do self-searching because we are "good enough the way we are" or "better than the next", which is a lie. The truth is, you are in constant need of examination and correction to varying degrees. That ol' pride creeps in very cunningly, and blinds you to your own faults. This is why you must look deeply and honestly into yourself and see what is really going-on, so others do not have to do this first. Many people will be there to point out your faults! Even if you have someone in your life – in prison – who cares enough, and has wisdom and experience to help you see the problems in your character that you are unable to recognize, you will still have to search yourself while being brutally honest about all you find.

Without a willing submission to this searching, those around you will be used to get you to see your shortcomings. The self-examination is painful, but not nearly as having a Brother in Christ correct you, or, even worse, an unbeliever. Let me be very clear: there are things in your character that have got to change. If you wish to be used to effectively minister where you are, you must be willing to ask God to reveal to you what needs to go and what must be added, now. If you have already seen and know some of these things, you need to allow the Holy Spirit to deal with them. I heard a Brother once say, **"The value of your work is dependent upon the character of your walk."** (Nocturn Show, Moody Radio)

The Book of Proverbs is filled with wisdom which is an excellent standard against which to analyze yourself and to show you what corrections need to be made.

Proverbs 1:7,"The fear of the Lord is the beginning of knowledge; but fools despise wisdom and instruction."

If we are willing to humble ourselves and receive correction from the Lord, sometimes through other Brothers, then we will grow and prosper in all we do, including our ministry. If we are unwilling (stubborn/rebellious), we will go nowhere fast, and experience problem after problem.

What I have seen all too often is men who do not take this seriously. Most grow tired of the consequences of their sin, including being on the losing-end of battles with the authority around them. The problem is, while men may tire of the effects, they do not tire of the sin itself. They do not turn to the Lord with a broken and contrite heart (one that is grieved because of the sin itself, not simply the consequence) and repent of their sins (are willing to give them up completely and turn from them), but still think they can somehow walk a "Christian" walk while holding onto the sin. This cannot ever work. You cannot love your sin and love God.

Read: *John 1:4-6,"He that saith, I know Him, and keepeth not His commandments, is a liar, and the truth is not in him."*

For what are we primarily seeking in our self analysis? Here is what the Apostle Paul said to the Church at Corinth.

II Corinthians 13:5, "Examine yourselves, whether you be in the faith; prove your own selves."

And also, the book of James says, *James 1: 21-25, "Wherefore lay apart all filthiness and superfluity of naughtiness, and receive with meekness the engrafted word, which is able to save your souls. vs.2,"But be ye doers of the Word, and not hearers only, deceiving your own selves." vs.23,"For if any be a hearer of the word and not a doer, he is like unto a man beholding his natural face in a glass." vs.24,"For he beholds himself, and goes his way, and straightway forgets what manner of man he was. vs.25, "But whoso looks into the perfect Law of Liberty and continues therein, he being not a forgetful hearer, but a doer of the work, this man shall be blessed in his deed."*

What did God mean here? He means, firstly, that if your faith is not properly placed in the Cross, you are walking in darkness (lost); you will be unable to see the defects in your own character, as well. When St. Paul said "the faith", he meant "Jesus Christ, and Him Crucified." This is the starting-point for everything. When your faith is in Jesus' finished work at Calvary for the answer to all your problems, then everything falls into place and you will be shown what changes need to be made. Is this painful at times? Yes! Is this a much wiser and better decision than having to be chastened (forcefully corrected) because of your pride and foolishness? Absolutely!

Analyze yourself against God's Word and allow the
Holy Spirit to make the necessary changes so you do not have to
experience the type of correction that comes from stubbornness,
pride, and foolish rebellion. Remember true change is only
found at the Cross.

No Shame in Saying, "I am Wrong"

You are not perfect. You are not closer to perfection
than anyone else! There will be times you are wrong; probably
many more than you would like to recognize and admit. Your
pride will tell you that you never need to admit this to others
when you see it in yourself, but this is a lie. In fact, if you do not
admit you are wrong, you will quickly be discovered as being
arrogant and phony. People will quickly accept your being
wrong at times, but they have no tolerance for someone who
will not admit he is wrong.

There is no shame in saying, "I am wrong" when you
are, but there is much shame in trying to say you are not wrong
when in fact you are. The same goes for telling others that you
are sorry for what you have done, as well as asking forgiveness.
What people need to see in you is honesty and earnestness
(serious intent), not someone who is too perfect to admit his
own shortcomings.

The more you practice repentance and humility, as soon
as you see wrong in yourself, the easier it gets to address your
mistakes. It is rarely ever "easy". When people around you see

this type of honesty in you, they will be that much more inclined to listen and receive from you the Gospel of Jesus Christ. Do not let the thing that turns them away be you! Do all you can to show them that you are an honest, humble person who makes mistakes at times, but does not hide behind dishonesty and lies. There is no shame in saying, "I am wrong."

Your Job as a Servant

Why are you here on earth? This question can be answered by saying: to serve the Lord by bringing Glory to God in all we do. In every conscious decision you make every second of every day, the primary motivation should be bringing Glory to God. Not part of the time, but all of the time. Remember, everyone is watching the Christian. This is a life of service, not a show to put-on. You will need a servant's heart. The Lord said in *Matthew 20:26-27, "Whosoever shall be great among you, let him be your minister. Vs. 27,"And whosoever will be chief among you, let him be your servant."*

The heart of a servant is the Spirit's work of regeneration. The world does not understand this concept; you will not see in on MTV, BET, Gangland, etc. The concept is mostly clearly demonstrated at the Cross, where Jesus was obedient unto death. While we are rarely called to die for the Gospel in the United States, we are called to be living sacrifices. This life of servitude is a high calling, in fact, the highest. Jesus continues His life of service to the Father through us.

Remember, on your own you will not have the strength, patience, humility, compassion, guidance, and love to carry-out this service. Daily, while you seek the Lord's heart at the foot of the Cross (the only place where He meets with fallen man), you will also find the strength to serve Him in the joy of the Lord.

So what does this service to the Lord include? We serve people's spiritual, emotional, mental, and physical needs, as ministers of the Gospel. In this chapter we will primarily cover the spiritual and emotional needs, because others are covered in separate chapters.

We, as Christians, have learned that spiritual health is far more important than the rest because it is the foundation of the others. If you are not spiritually healthy, you cannot be mentally or emotionally healthy, either. The physical will die eventually, no matter what. It's value lies in its use as a tabernacle for the Holy Spirit only. While we recognize this fact, lost people do not. In order to minister to their spiritual health, you will need to address, at times, their concerns for the other kinds of health first. This will enable you to gain their trust, undivided attention, and their gratitude.

Service to the Lord obviously includes sharing the Message of the Cross with others, and, includes walking a walk that draws men to Christ. But is that all? No, there is much more to it than that, but all you do should help you achieve those objectives as well.

With whom do you deal in ministry? It is people. It is not animals or robots or puppets, but people who need the Lord. Additionally, we deal with other Believers who need our help at times. One of the most important parts of your ministry is that of edifying and encouraging others. Men and women, no matter whom they are, need encouragement from you. Some are very insecure and have very little self-confidence, while others are at various stages of their developments and may not need as much attention as others. Everyone goes through times of struggle and doubt, even the Bible greats, like John the Baptist.

Matthew 11:1-3, "And it came to pass, when Jesus had made an end of commanding His Twelve Disciples, He departed thence to teach and to preach in their cities." vs 2, "Now when John had heard in the prison the works of Christ, he sent two of his disciples" vs 3, "And said unto Him, Are You He Who should come, or do we look for another?"

So a very important part of your ministry has to be bringing words of true encouragement; it will normally draw them to you. They will understand that you care about them enough to notice and say something of this nature to them.

You never have to, nor should you ever want to say something that is not true. There is enough to find in someone's life, if you honestly look, to bring-forth and acknowledge and/or compliment someone, so you never have to say anything that is untrue or exaggerated. Doing so will only backfire and work against you.

Aside from helping others, this service of love will help you to begin to look past people's obvious faults and offenses. You begin to value the soul and grow concerned for its eternal destination, and will move away from focusing on what is not pleasant for you to be around. Your job is to gain people's trust, and you should since you know the answer to their problems, the Cross of Christ. You can make this easier on yourself by helping them feel better about themselves; not to feel better in their sins, but to validate them each as a person --- show them Christian love --- so you can share with them the Gospel Message, and build a relationship.

When it comes to other Believers, your job is to edify them – build them up --- in the faith. Regardless of how badly Believers may behave at times --- and they will, your job is to "Bear all things, believe all things, hope all things, and endure all things." Why? Because "Love never fails". Put aside people's offenses and encourage them. Let them know that you see the good things in them, even if all you see at times is that Jesus is their Savior. Believers can be just as fragile as unbelievers (some even more so!), so you must keep this in mind and help them grow in God's grace. When people are discouraged, especially Believers, they will not grow at all.

There is no discouragement at the Cross. In fact, all of our victory is found there. That is why you must do your best to point others to this cure for all their problems. Unbelievers will not understand this, and that is why you need to explain the Gospel Message. Share with them the "Blessed Hope" that is available to all who will turn to Him. We do not make progress by "pushing and shoving" what we know to be true upon them, but we will make progress when we encourage others to seek the Lord as the answer to all of their problems.

Believers will be more likely to receive from you if you deal with them kindly and gently, as well, but even they may not fully understand that the Cross is the answer. It is your job, as directed by the Holy Spirit, to lead them to the only answer to mankind's problems.

Your job as a servant is to encourage those around you with the truth, and lead them to Jesus and what He did on the Cross. There is an old saying I heard years ago that always stuck with me: ***"People may not remember exactly what you did, or what you said, but they will always remember how you made them feel."*** People are emotional beings. Even though you have the answer to all their problems, which is the Cross of Christ, unless you handle your dealings with them humbly and wisely, they will build their walls. If you sincerely encourage them they will open up to you and become receptive. Again, it's not about being "right", it is about being effective. With God's help, you will become a fisher of men.

Encouraging others helps them to take their eyes off what is wrong in their life and/or with them, and gets them to focus on the solution: the Cross. Making someone understand that he is loved, cherished, and valued as a human being and as an individual by God and by you, His servant, is not flattery or deception. Flattery is not something to which a Christian need resort; deception is not a valid way of leading someone to the truth. People in prison are truly touched by someone who genuinely cares enough to reach out to them in their time of need. Because of men's pride, most find it difficult to request help from anyone. This is an opportunity for you, as a Christian, to really shine. When you take the initiative to reach out to others without being asked, it shows the sincerity of your care and compassion. This is one of the surest ways to lower people's defenses so they are receptive to you and your Message.

The Fruit of the Spirit

As I have said in many ways, if others do not see Christ in you, the ministry is a failure in God's eyes. As well, if His attributes are not seen in your life, then something is seriously wrong in your relationship with God. This is why the "YOU" part of this book had to come before other sections on "How To". The Fruit of the Spirit will only grow in your ministry if the Holy Spirit is free to work in your personal life. You give the Holy Spirit this freedom to do the work by having your faith anchored in what Christ did for you, not in your own performance.

Galatians 5:22-23, lists the Fruit of the Spirit. This is a list of qualities that should be evident in your life. They are qualities of the Holy Spirit, not of you.

1) **LOVE** – The Greek word that the Apostle Paul used here to describe this needed part of our character, is "agape" or "agapan". This is the same word translated as "Charity" in I Corinthians 13, which is also called the "Love Chapter". It means that it is a love called-out of a person's heart by "an awakened sense of value in an object which causes one to prize it." It is a love that recognizes the objects worth. In relation to ministry, this love is one that causes a person to recognize the value of someone's soul, and, thereby, will compel the person to do whatever sacrifice is necessary to build-up someone in the faith. This agape-love is the opposite of what the world offers, and it is self-less in nature.

Read I Corinthians 13, again until you get a full picture of what real love entails.

2) **JOY** – Joy is the outward manifestation of an inward peace. It is not dependent upon your circumstances, but instead, it should shine brighter under the pressures of trials and tribulations. It is how Paul said he could be "content in all his circumstances", because his joy abounded regardless of his hardships. When you are focused on Jesus and what He has done for you, you will feel joy bubble up inside of you. When you take your eyes off of Him and put them on your circumstance or problems, you will lose your joy. In ministry, joy is a must have.

Be aware; you do not just whip-up a batch of joy on your own or with others because it will not be a Fruit of the Spirit; it will be a fruit of your flesh, which is corrupt. You are to delight yourself in the Lord, not to derive your joy from the gifts He gives you (pleasures, comforts, niceties, etc.)

Psalms 37:4,"Delight yourself also in the Lord; and He shall give you the desires of your heart."

3) **PEACE** – This word describes the Fruit in your life that comes about only as you exhibit faith in what Christ has done for you on the Cross. Its meaning is not simply to be without worry; it is not a feeling, but an actual state of relation with God and man. It is tranquility from being in right relationship with God and man, a lack of hostility. The closer you draw to

the Lord, the more you will experience this peace. It, like the joy above, is not based upon circumstance, but on your relationship with Him.

4) **LONGSUFFERING** -- This word in the Bible means, "steadfastness of the soul under provocation". It means to be patient and to endure mistreatment and persecution, without anger or thoughts of revenge. The idea here is that God has been patient with you – suffered for a long time dealing with your foolish behavior and selfish rebellion – and you need to do the same with others. You know that, in prison, there are some very unique personalities with which to deal, so this area of your life really needs to be given to the Lord so He can lead you through. This patience is costly.

5) **GENTLENESS** – This describes a kindness that treats others very gently and without being harsh. This can be best seen in your forgiveness of others, as Christ has forgiven you, and in your not being defensive, offensive, or vengeful.

6) **GOODNESS** -- This quality which the Holy Spirit gives to you is seen in a man who is governed by, and strives for, what is good and right.

7) **FAITH** – Biblical faith is, first and foremost, faith in what Christ has accomplished for you on the Cross. However, faith, presented here as being a Fruit of the Spirit, speaks of your faithfulness when dealing with

others, and includes loyalty, trustworthiness, and dependability. It goes beyond simply being faithful to God during trials and tribulations, to being faithful to our fellow man, as well. It is, also, the highest level of responsibility between a husband and wife in a marriage. It could very well be translated as "trustworthiness" or "faithfulness".

8) **MEEKNESS** – This Fruit of the Spirit is a blend of both strength and gentleness. It is not "weakness", as some have thought it to be, mistakenly. It is one of the two words that the Lord Himself used to describe His Own character. That should be a big hint for you in your ministry, and something you will only receive by humbling yourself. It is the quality which allows you, while doing what is right and standing for the truth, to do so in love and gentleness. Meekness involves considering others before yourself. And when you truly care about where someone spends eternity, you will incorporate this into your ministry and life.

9) **TEMPERANCE** – This word describes the control over oneself that a Believer should possess. It is control over desires and impulses. Temperance is the yielding to the Holy Spirit's control of your thoughts and actions, and can only be accomplished by your faith being properly placed in what Christ has done for you at the Cross.

Forgiveness

This essential quality, which we have just seen as being linked to the fruit of the Spirit, is one that you had better learn how to do over and over. I have heard it well put that ministering to people, even just by the way you live your life and how you act and react, is somewhat like hugging porcupines. You put your loving arms around them while they cause you much pain. They are going to offend you, and at times slander you, give you attitudes, falsely accuse you, misrepresent what you do, assassinate your character, misquote you, and worse! Folks may even physically hurt you at times. However, your job is not to focus on the offenses committed against you, but to treat people well in return. This begins with forgiveness, if you have to. I say "if you have to" because after a while of learning how to handle offenses, many things will not even faze you in the slightest, but will only cause instant joy as you use the offense as an opportunity to show grace to them.

Understand this: in relation to what Jesus has forgiven you, you have no reason to ever not forgive someone who has done you harm in some way or the other, from the simplest to the greatest. Forgiveness is not about agreeing with what that person has done or saying "Oh, it doesn't matter". No, it means that despite what they did to you, you care enough to set the example, trusting in the Lord to use that situation to bring them to repentance.

In prison, you are not dealing with men who are known for their "superior moral qualities". They are people who have been stepped on and broken. They are hurting. Their past experiences and upbringing contribute to their acting out and being offensive. Do not get me wrong, they are still responsible for their actions and behavior, but it helps you to understand what goes on with them and why, so you can better minister to their need. If all you are doing is being offended by their behavior, then you cannot help them. You must first learn forgiveness, always, if you are going to be effective.

Matthew 6:14-15,"For if you forgive men their trespasses, your Heavenly Father will also forgive you. But if you forgive not men their trespasses, neither will your Father forgive your trespasses."

Effective Loving in Ministry

I know that I covered Love in the "Fruit of the Spirit" section, but this subject, as well as being "Joyous", requires some further explanation.

Learning to love others in prison can be a monumental task. It is definitely a crash-course. Only the Lord can teach you this, but, of course, there must be a willingness on your part to begin. The song says, "They will know we are Christians by our Love" and that is true. But how can you bring this "God kind of Love" about in your ministry? To start, it means putting God first, everyone else second, and yourself third. Mind you, this does not mean that you can run yourself ragged or neglect your own needs, especially, you must never neglect your personal relationship with God, the Father. God has to be your first Love. He must be foremost in your thoughts, feelings, desires, and values. When your relationship is satisfactory to Him, God will be equipping you, empowering you, and blessing you, caring for your every need. When you are walking in His perfect will, you will be assured every single need is met and this leaves you free to concentrate solely on the people to whom you are ministering. This is what Paul meant by:

Philippians 2:3-4, "let each esteem others better than themselves. Look not every man on his own things, but every man also on the things of others."

There is an attraction to genuine love that draws others, and this is what you want. You are not called to "like" everyone, but you are called to love them with the God kind of love. This means taking time to meet people at their point of need, and it means going out of your way, many times without being thanked. Your goal is not simply to go around doing "nice things", but eventually lead souls to the Cross and acceptance of Jesus Christ as their Savior and Lord. Before, during, and after, your ministry must be one of selfless love for others.

One of the ways you will be able to minister selflessly is in your giving. What are you going to need to give? One of the crucial things you must provide is (#1) *your time*. Ministry requires much sacrifice, and time is one of the most important. People will expect you to be there for them all of the time because you are the one to whom they look for answers. They may need something as simple as a scripture, or they may need help with a major problem of some sort. You have to do your best to help those around you when there is a true need, or even when you are simply cultivating the relationship, helping them build that trust in you. When you make yourself available to others you are letting them know that you value both them and their needs. It does not mean that you stretch yourself so thin that you do not have enough time for yourself, which you need, but it does mean that you make an extra effort for others in this area.

It will also be (#2) *your talents*. You have certain skills or knowledge that others will need at times, and part of relationship-building is using these talents to help others. Sometimes it will be to help the lost, and other times it will be to help fellow Believers; either way, you are called to help both. In fact, you are called to reach-out to all people, not just a select few. This does not mean that you will have the opportunity to share the Gospel with everyone, but it does mean that you work toward that goal by being kind and showing compassion, care and love.

Remember, the talents are to be used by the Holy Spirit. It is Him on whom you depend, not your talents. He instructs and guides in their use so you do not grow proud.

It will also include (#3) *your treasures*. You have to understand that God has not blessed you just so you can use all you have on yourself. In fact, much of what you have needs to be used in your ministry, if you are to be effective and see fruit produced. You have to learn what it means to truly give to others, while expecting nothing in return. This does not come naturally or easily to us in the flesh in which we live, but it is something that you must learn how to do. You must truly understand the importance of giving while expecting nothing in return. Once you see giving to others as it really is – an opportunity for you to bless and be blessed by the Lord – then you will look at life and your (God's really) passions in a whole new way. Just like a stone carver does not simply see a lump of granite as just being a rock, but what it has the potential to be, you will begin to see your giving as a way to minister to those around you.

In all my time of learning to give, which is still an ongoing process, I have never had the Lord disappoint me. He always takes care of my needs. You just have to be sure that you are giving correctly, with the right motive; you are not called to simply give your things away so you can be viewed as a "good person". On the contrary, you are called to be "a good steward" of the possessions that God has given you, which many times means you are to give as directed by the Holy Spirit.

The Word of God says in, *II Corinthians 9:6-7,"But this I say, He which sows sparingly shall also reap sparingly; and he which sows bountifully shall reap also bountifully"* *vs.7, "Every man according as he purposes in his heart, so let him give; not grudgingly, or of necessity: for God loves a cheerful giver."* When you give to others, give freely of the things you are giving, but as well, give freely of your joy when doing so. You never want others to feel guilty or indebted to you because of the way you gave to them, or because of your attitude not being one of care and joy. Be sure folks understand that you are happy to help.

This type of joyful giving will have an amazing effect. What I have found is that many men in prison equate someone's giving to them as a sign of love. Perhaps that is how a family member was able to show them love. Once you gain their trust, and they begin to understand that you really do care about them, then you are able to share the Message of the Cross. For Believers who already have some knowledge of the Message, you will be able to share more with them.

You cannot take anything with you when you leave this earth! Job said, *"Naked I came out of my mother's womb, and naked I shall return thither."* **(Job 1:21).** All that you possess must be viewed in light of your ministry. We are not to store up treasures for ourselves here on earth, but to use the things we have to further the Gospel and make disciples.

A word of warning: Although it is better to lean toward the side of giving when you do not know if it is the correct thing to do, you want to be wise in your giving, at all times. You are not called to give to those around you – especially men & women in prison - who have bad habits and bondages that they are not trying to correct. We are not to help others along in their sin (enable them). You would not give a drug addict money for his next fix simply because you want to "give". The same goes for an alcoholic, just so you can help him "ease the pain". Likewise, you are not called to give to those who spend their money and time on these vices, or others, by providing them with your food items, coffee, stamps, or whatever else. You must be a good steward of what you have. Although, there will be times that you will use such opportunities to share the Gospel with people, you do not support a bad habit *(sin)* but you can at times turn it to your advantage. Use wisdom when giving.

So how does love appear in your ministry? It stands out as your giving of yourself and your things, with joy, to further the Gospel and to bring glory to the Lord Jesus Christ. Be sure that when the Lord puts it on your heart to give, or you simply know that it's the right thing to do, that you take the time to point-out to others whom they should thank: the Lord. You are not here to steal the honor and glory due Him. The love expressed in your ministry is based on your love for Him.

Praise, Thanks, and Worship

Some of the most essential components of your living faith are praise, thanksgiving, and worship. Praise means: "to glorify, value, merit". It is derived from the word "prize". The scriptures tell us many, many times that God is *worthy* to be praised. "Worthy" says He merits praise that is due to Him. Praise is not something we offer only when everything seems to be in our favor, or we feel good! It is to be offered to God continually as He deserves. The psalmist said, **Ps. 110:4-5,** *"Enter into His gates with thanksgiving, and into his courts with praise: be thankful unto Him, and bless His name. For the Lord is good; His mercy is everlasting; and His truth endures to all generations:"*

Praise from the heart glorifies God, which is to be the predominant motive of every Born-Again Believer (Saint). Praise, the opposite of complaining, has the effect of refocusing our attentions from our struggles to the wonderful *MERCY* and *GRACE* of our loving Savior. Praise changes our attitudes, it restores our joy, which we forfeit so easily by complaining; this is a sign of the worst sin: unbelief. Isaiah told us that the Lord has given us *"the garment of praise for the spirit of heaviness:"* (61:3)

Incorporate praise into your every-day routine; to neglect this fundamental aspect of your Christian life will invariably lead you from God-consciousness to self-consciousness, rendering you powerless, helpless. Whether in thought, word, or song, praise is an opportunity and instrument from God which we must cherish and utilize constantly. *"Because Your loving kindness is better than life, my lips shall praise You"* (Psalm 63:3)

Thanks means "an expression of gratitude". Far too often neglected in the hearts and minds of Believers, thanks is the offering of your appreciation to the Lord for Whom He is, and what He has done. Giving thanks promotes humility by reminding the Believer (you) that he is most unworthy of God's gracious generosity. To complain is to believe that you deserve more or better than God has done or provided, and that, in your eyes, He is neglectful of His children, and a poor provider! This should never be! No one is more worthy of thanks than the Lord. Give God thanks! *"Therefore will I give thanks unto You, O Lord, among the heathen, and sing praises unto your name."* (Psalm 18:49).

"In every thing give thanks: for this is the will of God in Christ Jesus concerning you". (1 Thessalonians 5:18)

Worship means "to revere, to regard with great or extravagant respect, honor, or devotion". Many Believers are under the misconception that worship only occurs in church on Sunday, but in actuality, it is the lifestyle of devotion and service to God demonstrated by true disciples. This is why Jesus says: *"You hypocrites well did Isaiah prophecy of you, saying, this people draw near unto me with their mouth, and honor me with their lips; but their heart is far from me. But in vain they do worship me, teaching for doctrines the commandments of men."* (Matthew 15:7-9)

While praise and thanks are elements of worship, to be acceptable to God worship must be *"in Spirit and in truth"*. The Expositor's Study Bible says: "God is not looking for Holy Worship; He is looking for Holy Worshippers". Calvary makes this possible. As well, "..man worships the Lord through and by his personal spirit, which is moved upon by the Holy Spirit; otherwise it is worship God will not accept".

Praise, thanks and worship must never originate from the flesh. The Spirit of God will lead you in your worship of God and all of which it consists. The Holy Spirit (Fire!) is what makes Holy things Holy; it is He that sanctifies. *Never forget!* The only way the Holy Spirit can function fully in your life, as He is so willing to do, is if all your confidence and trust is in Jesus' Sacrifice on your behalf, not in your own works, self-will (determination), intellect, background, education, etc. The reason that God is willing to work in your life is that He is well-pleased with what Jesus has done, and your trust in it, not because of anything you have done, or could possibly do.

The Holy Spirit can glorify Jesus and the Father as you could never ever begin to imagine. Let Him do it through you.

When you are fully submitted your life will be worship. Praise God, He has done it all.

Being Joyous

Even though I have mentioned Joy earlier, it is important enough to single-out on its own. Being joyous is a way of life, not an act or reaction to circumstances. Your joy is based on your being "in Him". If those around you do not see joy in you, you will NEVER draw them to Christ. Who wants to follow a sourpuss? They are those who only want "religion", not the truth. The Bible is filled with the command (not a mere suggestion!) to rejoice. Why? To begin, God knows that your flesh lusts after focusing and dwelling on what is not good or pleasant in your life. In other words, you could be blessed with a new car and house today, and tomorrow your flesh will try to find things about which to complain. The same holds true when it comes to things of the Lord. After all God has done for you, you still want to focus on what you consider to be negative around you. It comes naturally to your fallen Sin Nature. This is why, as Believers who trust in the Lord, you focus on rejoicing as often as you can, not on things that are unpleasant and beyond your control. Do not ignore problems that seriously need your thought and attention, but do not dwell on the negative for no other reason than it is what you are accustomed to doing. You have too much about which to rejoice to do something that foolish. Besides, what are you really saying to the Lord when you focus on what is wrong and/or complain?

You are saying to Him, "I don't trust you, and what you've given me is not good enough."

Allow me to share with you this important lesson that I had to learn "the hard way": God hates complaining! You will tangle yourself up in your walk and in your ministry when you begin to complain. If you fall into this trap, repent immediately! Do not let it go any further. The Lord will not allow you to prosper as you should while you are stuck in this sin.

Here is what Paul said; *"Rejoice in the Lord always: and again I say, rejoice." (Philippians 4:4).*

This is for a reason, not by accident. Remember the Word says, *"The joy of the Lord is our strength." (Nehemiah 8:10)*

When you have un-confessed sin, such as pride, you will lose your joy and peace. Let this be a gauge for you to help you regain your joy when you lose it. Sometimes it is as simple as taking your eyes off the Lord and putting them on your problems. You need His joy daily-----every moment, as a Believer. And others need to see it in you if they are able to believe that He is real. People want to know what is real, and your life has to be a living testimony to the joy that He gives, so they know for sure that this lifestyle of joy is truly available to them right there in prison. Learn to rejoice in the Lord daily, and your life will change dramatically for the better, thereby affecting your ministry in a very powerful way.

God will give you favor in all things if you walk in Righteousness---His!

Matthew 6:33, *"But seek ye first the Kingdom of God, and His Righteousness; and all these things shall be added unto you:*, is a scripture that has helped me in my walk since I first learned its meaning. It is God's Word, so it must be heeded, and, as well, we can count on it to never fail.

In your ministry you are going to need the favor and power of God in all you do. Your power will not work, nor will God allow it to work. He does not share His Glory with your works. So it is essential that you seek the Kingdom of God----- His interests------and His Righteousness; then all you need in your life and ministry will be provided. (Not all you may necessarily want, but all you need).

Listen to what the Lord tells us: *"For You, Lord, will bless the righteous; with favor You will compass him as with a shield." (Psalm 5:12).* God's favor upon your life means He will shower you with gracious kindness, and partiality. It means that He will lift you and bless you before everyone to declare that you belong to Him. You want this in your ministry and so should every other servant of the Lord.

How does one seek and obtain the Kingdom of God and His Righteousness? By going to the Cross! The Cross is where you will find all things beneficial, wholesome, pure, etc., and it is the only place you find them. The Bible says that your righteousness-----your works on your own----- is viewed by God as "filthy rags" of the worst sort **(Isaiah 64:6).** Only His imputed Righteousness (Jesus' Righteousness credited to us) will be accepted, and it is not found within yourself, it is obtained by grace through faith. When you are "in Christ", by simple faith in Him and His sacrifice, God then gives you the Righteousness of Christ. It is the only true Righteousness that exists.

When you are walking in this "imputed righteousness", by faith, and you are obedient to what the Lord leads you to do through His word and His Holy Spirit, then God is going to open doors for you, mature you, give you favor in all things, and bless your ministry. There are many, many things you will need Him to do for you, including: going before you and preparing people's hearts before you speak with them; arranging situations so you can be effective while you minister; providing all materials you need; protecting you from the enemy; protecting others to whom you minister; providing your day-to-day needs, your health, etc.

Once you take your eyes off the Cross and put them on yourself and your own abilities, you frustrate the grace of God, thereby affecting your ministry and walk with the Lord.

Put God first and He will take care of the rest.

Getting Ahead of God

As a human, your nature is one to try to handle things yourself. You are very centered around "Self", and try to exert your "independence" whenever you can. You try to control things, while pushing God and His will out of the picture. This does not work in your walk, and it certainly will not work in ministry. Many times you do this without recognizing that you have done so. You may set out to do your best for Him, but you quickly run off in your own direction to do your own thing. You must always be on guard that you do not get ahead of the Lord. The moment you do, you are on your own, working out of your flesh. It is wasted time and energy that should be spent serving Him, His way, not your way.

So, how do you stay in step with the leading of the Holy Spirit, and not get yourself ahead of God? You let him make all the plans, and you simply follow them. You yield to the Holy Spirit so you can say *"nevertheless not my will, but thine be done":* as our Lord said, **(Luke 22:42).** Remember: if you are "resting", as you ought to be, you will not be tug-o'-warring with the Holy Spirit over decisions, because your will has been conformed to His. You should find God's will pleasant, enjoyable, and fulfilling.

Your ministry must be Spirit-led, and that means not letting yourself make decisions that He should be making. Again, do not ever make plans and ask the Lord to bless them! Let Him make the plans for you, and they will be blessed, already.

Putting Time Limits on God

Along with "not getting ahead of God", is "not putting Him under your time constraints or conditions". The first interferes with His Will, and the second with His timing. Both of them are equally important. God does not work for you or me, so it is Him to Whom we need to listen. I have seen many men who have put themselves on the path of disappointment because they believed that they could somehow get God to do things in their timing. A number of those men did so naively. Still others fell into the deception of the "Word of Faith" teaching, thinking they could confess things into existence. Either way, disappointment and trouble soon arose, with many drifting away from the truth. It is the height of foolishness to think that you, an imperfect, fallen human being, can somehow know how to arrange things such as timing, better than God. I have seen this happen most in the area of men's desire to be free from prison. Let me be very clear, so you will know the truth: *DELIVERING YOU OR ANYONE ELSE FROM PRISON IS NOT GOD'S PRIMARY FOCUS!* Delivering you and everyone else from sin is His all consuming objective. Put your trust in the fact that God knows all about your situation---even arranging and using all your bad choices---while your job is to allow Him to prepare you day by day. You then begin to reach-out to others and draw them to Jesus. Allow Him to teach you patience as you realize that scriptures such as, *"Be still, and know that I am God: (Psalm 46:10)* are for you today, just as they were for Israel of old. No one said that this ministry would be easy, but if you want all God has for you, including a powerful ministry that glorifies the Lord and brings souls to Jesus, then you will learn humility and patience.

"Wait on the Lord: be of good courage, and He shall strengthen your heart: wait, I say on the Lord." (Psalm 27:14)

"Rest in the Lord, and wait patiently for Him." (Psalm 37:7)

Your Prayer Life

We now come to a part of your life and ministry that, if overlooked or neglected, will leave you weak and powerless. Prayer is a tool that God gives to us so we can have a direct part in the work that He does. You must understand that God does not need your prayers; you need Him to answer them. As time passes, He will teach you what to pray so He can align your will with His.

A ministry not based on prayer is like a car's trying to run without gasoline. It goes nowhere. How can you without the leading and guidance of the Holy Spirit? You must be disciplined in this area if you hope to be effective. Is not that really the point? If you are not about doing your best, then why bother? Set aside time each morning to spend with the Lord! (We are not under law, but do this!!!) Find at least 15-20 minutes that you can use to pour-out all of your love and appreciation, as well as your cares and worries to Him, while asking guidance in all areas. Pray for those around you, including staff members. Ask God to give you wisdom and understanding so you can serve Him better (be used to a greater degree). Ask Him to give you a greater burden for the lost souls, and ask Him to lead you to them. Ask Him for proper interpretation of His Word: clarity of vision for your life; for laborers for His harvest; that you enter not into temptation; for wisdom and obedience for those in government and authority; for peace in Jerusalem, etc.

What I have found is this, also: God will many, many times, use things in our lives to slow us down and get us to focus on our prayer life and studies. Not long ago I began experiencing constant headaches, the likes of which I had not previously encountered. After a series of attempts to try to rid myself of them, and a number of weeks going by with their not letting up, I began to realize that God had answered one of my prayers. I had prayed for a stronger prayer life, and this situation literally drove me to my knees. Had I simply complained and carried-on, I would not have seen His Hand in it at all. Today I am grateful for the headaches. My prayer life increased, and He gave me the grace to make it through the worst of them. Since that time I have seen the effect of my prayers in many areas. The Lord was showing me the power of prayer beyond what I had previously known. I may be a blood-bought child of the King, but I still need some forced discipline at times. Although God uses many ways to get His children to learn lessons, it is because He loves us, not because He is punishing us. He knows what is required to get our attention. Some learn easily. Others, like I at times, need the stick, not the carrot.

On the subject of personal prayer, allow me to explain the meaning of praying with understanding, and also praying in the spirit. Praying with understanding is either vocal or silent prayers that are specific; you understand exactly for what you are praying. It is an opportunity for you to participate in God's Work through your prayers, as well as to build your faith, and helps you to become familiar with God and His Ways. Some answers will be "yes", some "no", and some "wait". The answers of "yes" and "no" will teach you God's values, and you will learn to discern what is good for you, and what is harmful. The answer, "wait" will teach you to trust in God's timing. To pray with understanding will not change God's mind or will; it will conform your will to His. This is the goal, to be like Jesus.

Praying in the spirit, also known as "praying in tongues", is the prayer language a Believer receives upon being baptized with the Holy Spirit. This type of prayer, which is for personal edification, allows you to experience His refreshing and rest that He promised in **Isaiah 28:12.** Reality is, we do not even really know what we need in the overall picture. This is why Paul told us in **Romans 8:26,** *"Likewise the Spirit also helps our infirmities; for we know not what we should pray for as we ought; but the Spirit itself makes intercession for us with groaning which cannot be uttered."* As you experience this blessing your relationship with the Lord will grow more intimate.

Your prayer life is one of utmost importance to you as a Believer, and even further when you are in ministry. Your flesh will fight you and make excuses why you do not need to pray, and to justify putting it off. Make a decision to incorporate prayer into your day. You will begin to see great results very shortly, as well as many prayers answered years after you lift them up to the Lord. Hallelujah!

Remember, God loves us and wants to answer our prayers. We just need to be sure they are in accordance with His Will, and that we trust Him fully to answer them the best way, which is always what He does. Our job is to have that full confidence in Him that He will do it in is His timing.

"And this is the confidence that we have in Him that, if we ask anything according to His Will, He heareth us: And if we know that He heareth us, whatsoever we ask, we know that we have the petitions that we desired of Him." (1 John 5:14-15)

Do not neglect prayer, and do not be afraid to ask God for His Will to be done in your life in all areas. Satan will try to make you afraid of doing so, but do not listen to his lies. God's Will is always best for us (Note: if you pray poorly, ask the Lord to teach you how, and He will).

Prayer Groups

Prayer groups are popular in jails and prison, and many of the prayers are about the prisoner's cases and freedom. While there is nothing wrong with praying for these things, and those prayers may even be necessary at times, your focus needs to be on being delivered from sin and walking with the Lord, not on how quickly you can get out of prison. This is why you, as a

Christian in ministry, need to conduct proper prayer groups, as a leader. I have been in too many prayer groups where people either ramble on and on about things when it comes to their turn, or simply never put prayers forward, and only list a thousand things for which they say they desire to give thanks in their life. Although there is certainly not anything wrong with thanking the Lord, that should not be the primary objective in these groups unless it is thanks and praise for prayers put forth in the group or testimony to recently answered prayers in one's individual prayer life. Let the prayer group be a time of putting forth *specific, brief* prayers from those attending so, when the prayers are answered, the answers will be recognized and used to glorify the Lord, as well as build-up the Believer's faith. When the men in the group begin to see that God really answers prayers—thereby showing that He truly loves His children and upholds His Word—their faith begins to grow. You, as a prayer-group leader, need to gently push the men in the right direction by keeping the prayer group structured; not unbendable or stiff, but structured so the members can learn to pray properly in a group and see God's Hand moving. Remember, you are a leader, and need to exhibit gentle but firm control, otherwise, the members begin to dread coming either because it takes too long to go around the prayer circle/group or because they simply see no results.

Prayer groups are also excellent tools to help you witness to others. There are too many instances for me to recall the number of men I have encountered who, at the outset, started voicing to me their negative opinions of Christians and/or Christianity, only to later approach me and ask "can you please pray for my mom" or "dad", or whichever loved one is having a problem. When you let people know that you are praying for them, it touches their heart. They realize that you care about them, and it opens the door for you to share with them the truth: the Message of the Cross. Prayer groups are excellent for bringing the petitions of the unsaved, or those who simply do not attend, to the Lord in front of the Believers who do participate. While God is under no obligation to answer the prayers of the unsaved, He does answer His children. The person for whose situation you promised to pray is grateful, and those in the group get to see God's moving as well. What you will begin to see is many people come looking for you, saying "Thank you so much, my situation changed", or however they say it, because God glorifies Himself and they see that your prayers on their behalf were answered.

I must warn you, however: prayer groups, like many other things in your walk with the Lord and your ministry, are a commitment and a sacrifice because there will always be other things going on at the prison that will try to draw you away from the group. You do not have to be legalistic about it, but be structured and committed. You never know what type of situation someone may be facing in which you and the prayer group are the only hope of which the person knows. It may appear to just be a "small prayer group", but there is a big responsibility that accompanies it. There is also great reward. Prayer can be an exciting time of fellowship and growth if you allow it to be.

You must keep in mind that a prayer group is not to be used for prayers and communication that you are to have with the Lord in your personal time with Him. Although your prayers may be personal in nature, you want to keep the focus on issues/requests of which the others will be able to hear and see the results when they are answered. Again, it is not a time of simply saying "I just want to thank the Lord for waking me up this morning"! Be specific in your prayers! Do not be afraid to ask God for specific things. When your will is aligned with His, you can expect results. God longs to answer your prayers in the best way possible. He even tells you in **James 4:2** that you, the Believer, miss out on so much because you do not go to Him with your requests.

So use the prayer groups to glorify God by putting forth your petitions and trusting that He will answer.

As a leader, do not be afraid to structure the group and let others know what is expected, such as being brief and specific. You do not have to rush, and you want the members to put forth all for which they wish to pray, but at the same time you want to be respectful of the time and the others in the group. If people do not have a request, tell them to move on to someone else. You should not be searching for something to pray at the last minute. Let the men know that, but be wise and gentle in how you do so.

Keep in mind, prayer is not about talking God into something or changing His mind. You can do neither. Prayer changes *our* hearts and minds. God is unchanging (immutable), and all wise and knowing (omniscient). When we converse with God, our desires, thoughts, and traits do not "rub-off" on Him; we are the ones who are conformed to His image, and His ways become ours.

Fellowship

Fellowship is one of the greatest blessings that you will experience as a Believer, and in ministry those blessings will be amplified if you fellowship scripturally.

Fellowship is the gathering together of Believers for companionship, a community of interest, activity, or experience. As Christians, this is essential to our growth. Believers assembling together on one accord can be a tremendous blessing. The Bible says that *"Iron sharpens iron; so a man sharpens the countenance of his friend"* (Proverbs 27:17).

Fellowshipping is a "must" for you if you are to grow, but fellowship is not always easy. You may not always agree with or even like a fellow Believer. This is where wisdom must be used. You may not like the attitude of someone who says he is a Christian, or even what he does, but, perhaps through your interaction, with your reaching-out to him in love and kindness, you can help him to see the need to change on his own. It does not mean that you are called to spend all your time with that person, but if you can reach out to him at times, you should. You know it is easier to be around other Believers with whom you "get along" well, but you must not stop there. Reach-out in love. Show that you care about a person who may be offensive at times. You can make a difference in his life! Many times it just requires spending some time with others so they can see the humility and love in you. If you, a minister of Jesus' love, are not willing to make that sacrifice, something is very wrong. Our lives are about bringing others to Christ, and building them up afterward.

I must warn you, however; you are neither called to fellowship with others who do not stand for the truth, nor those who live in willful sin. We as Believers are not called to "come-together" in unity, but in truth. Prison is no different. Light and darkness are not to have fellowship! God tells us also, *"Wherefore come out from among them, and be ye separate, saith the Lord, and touch not the unclean thing; and I will receive you"* (2 Corinthians 6:17)

Fellowshipping with other servants of the Lord will build you up as you do the same to them. It will also keep you away from those who desire to tempt you and lure you into the ways of the world. Fellowshipping is extremely important.

Here is what I have seen in prison happen to those who have been committed to fellowship: they grow in grace and God uses them. They are held accountable by each other, which takes away the option of hiding their sin and ways which are not pleasing to the Lord. Commitment is required to do this. Not everyone who claims the name of Christ really desires to grow. Many simply fool themselves into thinking that in prison "Christianity" is an easier path. It is not! It is the toughest walk a man can choose in prison. You are under the watchful eye of everyone around you. Those who do not really serve the Lord will quickly buckle under pressure. They expose themselves as being something they're not, and, simultaneously, they put a stain on the real servants.

Also, I have observed in those who are not committed to fellowship: that they stop growing in the Lord and they *quickly* move backward. No fellowship ---- no growth. From where does this stem? Pride! No Christian who serves the Lord and loves his Brother isolates himself. Such is love for "Self", not for the Brothers, nor the Lord. The Lord said, *"If you love Me, keep My commandments"* **(John 14:15)**

"This is my commandment, that you love one another, as I have loved you." **(John15:12)**

The Lord said, as well: *"Behold, how good and how pleasant it is for brethren to dwell together in unity. It is like the precious ointment upon the head that ran down upon the beard, even Aaron's beard: That went down to the skirts of his garments;"* **(Psalm 133: 1-2)**

"And let us consider one another to provoke unto love and to good works: Not forsaking the assembling of ourselves together, as the manner of some is; but exhorting one another: and so much the more, as you see the day approaching" **(Hebrews 10:24-25)**

These are God's commandments. You do not listen to your flesh; you listen to Him. This next illustration will help you to see what happens to a man who removes himself from fellowship. If you see a campfire burning brightly, piled with logs, and you pull one of those logs from the flames and put it off to the side, it will still burn for a little while longer. Not too long after, however, its flames disappear, and it stops burning. In order for that log to burn---to let its light shine--- it must be together with the other logs. In your walk with the Lord, you must have fellowship with other true Believers if you are to keep shining as well. The moment you isolate yourself (and this normally happens because of pride and un-forgiveness), you set yourself up to fall. Do not fall into this trap!

What type of fellowship are you to have? You can fellowship with other Believers in many ways. Bible study is one way, as well as just sitting in your cell and talking. You can play sports and fellowship, as well as eat together. A few times a year we even hold camp meetings in our cells and provide food and beverages as we listen to services over the radio. Just make sure that whatever you do is done for God's glory.

One last word about fellowshipping: Yes the Bible says *"Iron sharpens iron"*. We know this to be true because the Lord says so. But we also know that there are sparks in this process. This is natural at times. Simply do your best to treat those around you with respect, and always be willing to humble yourself. You must value the relationship and not let something such as a disagreement break your fellowship. Brothers are going to offend each other. When you recognize this, be quick to humble yourself—even if you have been wronged or offended—and make things right with the Brother. Set the example. As a leader, you need to.

Ministry is not the Lord's primary desire for your life. Christian life is about relationships. The relationship with God is clearly before every other. However, the Bible plainly teaches, if your relationship with your Brother is strained or broken, your relationship with God is equally broken. If there is bad blood between you and God's child, there is bad blood between you and God. **(See I John 3: 15-18, 4:20-21)**

The Bible says that you cannot hate men and love God. God is far less interested in your outward behavior (ministry) than in the attitude of your heart toward other people. Even if you are the victim of the situation, remember, it is not about you. Jesus died for that person. Your comfort and feelings are going to be sacrificed many times over for the glory of God and the edification of the Body (this does wonders for your pride!). Your immediate focus needs to be healing the wounds and restoring the fellowship with everyone involved.

Lust: Setting the Example

Aside from pride, no other sin will destroy your testimony like lust will. If this area is a struggle for you, you need to deal with this in the way God has prescribed: by looking to the Cross for your deliverance. You cannot have a ministry in prison or elsewhere, and be in bondage to lust. Make no mistake, it *will* take you down. Not only will you be exposed in *this* area, but no one will want to listen to your talk about the Lord, sin, deliverance, repentance, the Cross, etc., when they see that you are bound by lust. If you think for one moment that people are not watching you as you look at scenes/commercials on television, or at magazines, or even female guards, you are fooling yourself. You need to make a serious choice in this area of your life if you wish to serve the Lord. You cannot have it both ways, and the path to lust will only lead to destruction.

Also, sexual lust is not the only type of lust, though it is the most obvious at times. If you lust for material goods your stance/love for the Lord will be questioned, also. Worldly people may not know everything about what a Christian should do, but they are quick to recognize what a Christian *should not* do. Although your aim is not to please them, but the Lord, you still have to realize that how you're perceived by people matters. Seeing a Christian caught in lust makes those watching think that person is a fake, which is the complete opposite of your goal. Either you are here to serve the Lord, or you are simply serving your "Self". Do not discredit the Lord's Ministry with blatant hypocrisy. Surrender your lusts or quit. You are fooling no one. Everyone can see if you are living a life of lust. Bear in mind, this is a fight of faith. Although this weakness is built-in and deeply ingrained, if you do not believe God can deliver you, and trust He will, you will never be able to walk the walk, so stop talking the talk.

As time goes on we see a much greater push by the forces of evil to tempt man. This comes about in many ways, including movies produced, books written, magazines, television, through a society that strays further from God's Word, and even especially in the "church". You must carefully screen what you allow through your eyes, ears, and mouth. Your walk and testimony are at stake. Today we find so-called Christian Ministries that promote all kinds of ungodly lusts, including money and material goods, as well as youth–group gatherings which use worldly music and allow through this the type of "bump and grind" dancing that the average night club has. The purpose of gathering for church is not to promote sin, but to be delivered and remain free from it!

Everything in ministry rises or falls on leadership. If you, a leader, set a poor example of falling prey to lust, then to whom are the followers going to look? You are called to be a living sacrifice, which the Bible says is your *"reasonable service"* **(Romans 12:1).** Do not let lust destroy your testimony and ministry.

Personal Study

In time, more and more people will begin to look to you for answers to Biblical questions, as well as for overall counsel in what to do and how to live for the Lord. To not know the answer to their question can be a real hindrance at times. Though people understand that you may not know everything about the Bible, part of your ministry is to know as much as you can. This is why your personal study of the Word has to be a daily part of your life. This is a serious commitment that anyone who desires to have an effective ministry will make. The world is full of false information and deception that attacks the Word of God. You, as a servant of the Lord, must *"Be ready always to give an answer to every man that asks you for a reason of the hope that is in you with meekness and fear:* **(1 Peter 3:15)**

Unless you are devoted to daily personal study, you will neither be able to understand the Bible yourself, nor answer the questions of others properly. If you do not know the answer to a question, be honest and tell the person that you will find it for him. There is no shame in not knowing because you simply have not encountered that question previously. However, there is much shame in not knowing because you have neglected to put the time and effort into personal study.

Where do you start in this area? My suggestion, and one which I urge you to take, is to start by purchasing and reading /studying an Expositor's Study Bible, which is available from J.S.M. No other Study Bible currently available will aid you as this one will. No other even comes close! After years of my own studies using other popular Study Bibles, I have put them all aside in preference of the Expositor's. After just a few moments of reading one you will understand why. It will open your eyes to the scriptures in a way you never previously experienced. The Expositor's will help you to see and understand how the entire Bible is, from start to finish, the Message of the Cross; Jesus Christ and Him Crucified.

I counsel you very strongly: To not utilize the Expositor's Study Bible will impede your growth and ministry. I realize that these are strong words, but I stand behind them fully.

Next in line in your personal study material I firmly encourage you to obtain a number of study guides from the Cross of Christ Series, also available at J.S.M. "The Sin Nature" and "God's Prescribed Order of Victory (Romans 6)" guides are an excellent place to begin. Your spiritual growth and understanding will be multiplied many times over as you begin to comprehend these Biblical principles.

As well, I highly recommend J.S.M.'s commentaries on the books of the Bible, and the books they offer which deal with

107

people's questions. All of these materials are excellent, and I believe, from experience, tremendously helpful to Christian growth. If it sounds as though I am biased towards J.S.M.'s material, it's because I am. Once you find the best, you stick with it. That's not to say that there are not other books out there that are very helpful and insightful, but that my strong recommendation is that you start with what I have found to be the best.

How much time should you devote to personal study each day? There is not one particular answer to that question, but this I can tell you: you are in prison. You are in a place where you have plenty of time to spend studying. Even if you have a full-time job while you are locked-up, neither that job nor anything else should supersede your studies. Too tired to study each day because of the job? Quit! Find something else that allows you to both work and study. Your studies have to be a priority in your life. The only thing that should compare is your personal prayer life.

Since you have plenty of time, there is no reason why you cannot spend at *least* an hour or more on your studies. This will require discipline on your part, but if that is what your heart desires, you will accomplish the goal.

Do not, under any circumstances, turn your "discipline" into "legalism"! Here is the difference: With "legalism", your motivation is to gain merit or favor in God's eyes; with "discipline", your motivation is to please God because you love and trust Him. The difference between the two could not be greater.

I have seen far too many people fool themselves into thinking that they have to study some set amount each day (an amount they invent in their minds) or God will not be pleased. Others think that by studying more they are somehow pleasing God. Be very clear on this point: the only thing pleasing to God is our faith being placed in what Jesus has already done for us at the Cross! No amount of Bible study or prayer or church attendance, etc., will please Him. Those things can be very beneficial if done correctly, but they cannot somehow impress God. If you are studying His Word each day to be the "good boy", you are misguided. You earn *nothing* in God's eyes by doing so. However, if you are studying because your heart is right and you have a hunger to get to know Him through His Word better each day, then you are on the right track.

God is not "won-over" somehow by your puny efforts. Most of what calls itself Christianity still thinks that we are righteous and holy through our own efforts. Make no mistake: our righteousness and holiness come to us exclusively by grace, through faith in what Christ did. Things like prayer and reading God's Word can quickly be turned into a work or an idol if we do not understand this truth. So studying for three hours a day does not make you holier than if you studied for only two. You may learn more, but that is far different from holiness and righteousness.

Be committed to personal study because you want to grow in knowledge of His Word so you can love Him better and experience all He has done for you. There is great benefit to devoting yourself to this. Just be sure you do not allow it to become a chore or work. You will soon become disinterested and move away from it.

Legalism

What is legalism? The dictionary defines legalism as "strict literal or excessive conformity to the law or to religious or moral code." How does this apply to you? Your walk with the Lord will be greatly hindered by allowing forms of legalism to interfere. The word "legal" pertains to law. The suffix "-ism" shows that it is a belief. So we can say that legalism is, in regards to Christianity, a belief that we in some form need to keep or uphold the law. What law? This means any law that our minds concoct, including existing ones. What do I mean by that? Simply that we do not impress God by trying to keep the law: any law! In case you have not realized it yet, you cannot. Only Jesus kept the law perfectly, and it is only our faith in that perfect life and Sacrifice for us that God will accept.

Understand: Jesus kept the law flawlessly. It is in His performance we trust, not our own. When our faith is in Him, God imputes Jesus' sinless perfection to us, thereby making us keepers of the law in His sight. Your efforts cannot add to Jesus' perfection, they can only contaminate it.

Both men in prison and free men try to put one another under law. They will tell you that you cannot do this and that you have to do that, else you will "miss-out" on "your blessing". The rules they insist you follow are usually ones that they "make-up"! As well, Believers who do not understand the Message of the Cross and God's grace will even put themselves under law. This means that they make a law of going to church, of reading the Bible, of praying so many hours a day, etc. What I have seen is these "legalists" tell other people that they can or cannot do certain things that the legalists say will put their listeners in "bad standing" with God, as if the legalists were His spokesmen.

The issue of whether or not someone should bring food out of the chow hall seems to always be a point of focus for these legalists, with most usually breaking their own 'laws'. They tell others that it is sin in God's eyes to bring out a packet of sweetener, but they themselves buy all they can from kitchen workers who bring food back to the units. Not only is this legalism, but it is hypocrisy.

While I certainly do not advocate stealing, neither do I promote legalism. Whatever you do make sure you are not bringing shame to the Gospel. There may be certain things at your prison that staff allows/overlooks but is against their handbook policy. Be wise in what you do. Someone with an honest heart may have trouble pointing a finger at a person who takes a dessert (or whatever) back to his unit/cell-block from his own tray, but being stopped, searched and found with excessive food or other items will only damage your testimony.

If you think that obeying all the "rules" very strictly in prison is going to make you a better Christian (or perhaps more realistically, making you *think* you are better than the other Christians), then go ahead and try. You will fail. This walk is not about "keeping the law". No, I am not suggesting that you purposely try to break the rules where you are, but, after having experienced many situations over many years in prison, I will say this: many rules come and go. If you had tried to "keep them perfectly" you would barely be able to leave your cell. Be wise. Bring no shame to the Gospel. This walk is not about trying to be perfect, it is about keeping our faith in what Christ did on the Cross for us. Do not frustrate the grace of God by thinking you can somehow keep all of the "rules/laws" perfectly. When you hear people teaching this type of legalism, then stay away from the teaching (teacher)! This is put forth by prideful men who desire to control others, or simply just "religious men" who are set on trying to show you how "righteous" they are by their works. It is idiocy and should be avoided at all costs.

Legalism is about trying to keep the law. It is an insult to Jesus for you to base your hopes on this. You cannot have it both ways; it is either Jesus Christ and Him Crucified, or it is your works or trying to keep the law, impress God. The former produces victory in our lives, the latter produces failure.

The entire book of Galatians is devoted to the issue of law vs. grace, and how Believers are not to be entangled again in bondage of law. This is not saying or implying that we have a license to now sin, as some have accused, but rather freedom to serve God properly.

Tithing and Freewill Offerings

One of the greatest blessings and opportunities that the Lord has given us is the ability to tithe. The word "tithe" means "a tenth", and as most know, it means giving a tenth of what God has given you back to Him. Why do we do this? Firstly, we do this because God has instructed us to do so. Although the word "tithe" is not in the New Testament, the concept and example surely is.

Tithing is an opportunity that we have to use what we have been given to further the Gospel. Tithing is not about giving money away, buying something nice for someone, feeding hungry people, or anything else outside of spreading the Message of the Cross. At times you may need to feed people or meet their immediate need in order to be able to share the Gospel with them. However, meeting their physical needs with your tithing is only to be done so you can meet their spiritual need, which is the Gospel.

If you look at tithing as a chore you have to do to please God, then you might as well not bother. You should be grateful to be able to tithe, regardless of how much or how little you are tithing. Think about this: the Creator of the universe, the Lord of Glory, has given you an opportunity to help spread the most important Message ever given to mankind! Do you want to complain about being able to participate? No wise man would.

Whether you are tithing with your income or also with your talents and treasures, you must realize that all you have belongs to Him anyway. A tenth is a very small amount for God to tell you to return when He has given you the entire amount. These are two ways that God uses tithing in your life: to break you from the sin of greed, and to help you learn to trust Him fully. On your own, you would not give a penny. Your flesh can find a million reasons and excuses why you need to keep your measly money, but your trust ought never to be in money, your material possessions, or in your talents. It is God and Him alone, that you are to trust.

When you tithe you are being obedient. When you do not you are sinning against Him. What type of sin? To begin with, it is the sin of pride and rebellion. Make no mistake about it: God is going to get His tithe from you one way or the other. You can willfully give it to Him and receive His wonderful blessing upon your life, or you can have Him take it from you in a way that a wise person would not wish to have happen. The choice is yours.

When you give to God's work, His way, you enjoy His favor and blessing. If not, you are robbing God. Listen to what His Word tells you:

"Will a man rob God? Yet you have robbed Me. But you say, wherein have we robbed You? In tithes and offerings." (Malachi 3:8)

God is very clear on this subject. He calls it robbery to not participate in giving to Him and His work. As a Believer you do not want to miss out on this. Doing things the way He tells us to is always best.

Listen to what He says to those who will be obedient in this area of their lives:

"Bring ye all the tithes into the storehouse, that there may be meat in My house, and prove Me now herewith, saith the Lord of Hosts, if I will not open you the windows of

Heaven, and pour you out a blessing, that there shall not be room enough to receive it." **(Malachi 3:10)**

A word of warning to you in the area of tithing: Be sure that the people you entrust with God's tithes are preaching the Message of the Cross. What you support is equally important as the support you give. There is an abundance of so-called ministries/churches out there today that preach "another gospel" and "another Jesus", using the money they receive to line their own pockets or promote some sort of social program about which the Bible says nothing. You harm the work of God when you support this foolishness in any form or fashion. If you are not backing the truth, you are backing a lie.

Above and beyond your tithe, the Bible instructs you to offer what are called "freewill offerings" to the work of God, as well. Why? Because He has given you, through this, an even greater opportunity to support the Gospel, learn to trust Him even more, be broken from your dependency upon yourself and money, and to receive His blessing. God will never ask you to sacrifice something without having something else in store for you that is infinitely better. God does not need your money. Tithing is set-up for you, not Him. You must understand that.

This is what the Word of God says: *"But this I say, He which sows sparingly shall also reap sparingly; and he which sows bountifully shall reap also bountifully.*

"Every man according as he purposes in his heart, so let him give; not grudgingly, or of necessity: for God loves a cheerful giver.

"And God is able to make all Grace abound toward you, that you always having all sufficiency in all things, may abound to every good work:" **(2 Corinthians 9:6-8)**

I want you to understand it is not your finances that concern God, but your attitude. Your heart should feel indebted and thankful to God. Everything that you have should be at His disposal. The practice of tithes and offerings is a way to contribute to the spreading of the Gospel through the time and efforts of others. Tithes and offerings are a reminder to your greedy little heart that you are not to hoard (stash, lay up) money as an insurance policy in case God does not come through for you. He always does. If it costs you some of your personal comforts, good! The flesh is the enemy of God, so do not spend all God's money making it comfortable!

Becoming Familiar With What Those Around You Believe: Understanding "Religion"

In order for you to effectively share the truth with others you must understand their belief, what they have been told. Everyone believes in something, so you, as a minister of the truth, must familiarize yourself with many common beliefs to better show others who do not know the truth what the truth is. Unless you understand their background, you will find it a very difficult task to convey to them what is true and what is not.

How can you lead a Muslim to the Jesus of the Bible if you do not know the "Jesus" that he has been taught? How can you help a Mormon understand that Mormonism is not Christianity if you do not know what the book of Mormon tells him? How can you explain the power of God to a Jehovah's Witness if you do not know that he thinks that Jesus did not die on a cross and that their belief is that Jesus is not God but Michael the Archangel? How can you show the world that every religion/philosophy taught is, in reality, an invention of man, not God? (i.e.Buddhism, Taoism, Roman Catholicism, Shintoism, Gnosticism, Atheism, etc.).

In order to be successful in leading others to the truth, you must spend time studying the religions of the world, but before you do this, you must know why Biblical Christianity is not a religion. You must also realize that religion of any sort is the greatest enemy of God and mankind that exists today. Why? Because religion is a placebo—a fake pill that claims to cure our ills. Religion poses as being of God but, in fact, is a scheme of Satan to fool the people. And it works! *Religion makes people feel good all the way to Hell!* As Brother Swaggart had said so well, "Religion is the most powerful narcotic known to man." Religion masks the pain of conviction of sin while patting the sinner on the back and saying "good job". It is the terrible evil of the world which has been responsible for sending more souls to Hell than anything else man has encountered, including alcohol, drugs, pornography, war, etc. For you to be able to lead others away from this evil and into the truth, it is extremely helpful for you to know what they believe.

So what is Christianity, if it is not a religion? Plainly and simply, Christianity is a relationship with God through Jesus

Christ. In order to get to God you must go through the Cross. The religions of this world will tell you that there are other ways to get to God. They are lying. Buddha, Mohammad, Mary, the Saints, Confucius, Ellen G. White, Joseph Smith, C .T, Russell, Norman Vincent Peale, L. Ron Hubbard, nor any other religious leader has ever saved a soul from Hell. Only the Lord Jesus Christ can and will do that.

Religion, which is fully the brainchild of Satan, embraced by man, is man's rebellious attempt to reach God or to somehow better himself by his own efforts and good works. The world calls it wonderful, while God calls it wicked and evil. In contrast, the Gospel—The Message of the Cross—is God's plan to reach fallen man. "The Gospel" means "Good News", and for those who truly desire to be forgiven and are willing to choose God over their sin, it is the "Best News".

To be a Christian means that you have been Born-Again, spiritually. It does not mean that you go to church. It does not mean that you read your Bible. It does not mean that you pray. It means you have been washed clean by the precious Blood of the Lord Jesus Christ, and that you now belong to Him. It means you are now a child of God **(see John1:12).** Am I saying that you should not go to church, read your Bible, or pray? Of course not! Those things can be very helpful, and will be if correctly done. However, they do not make anyone a Christian.

When you hear people of other beliefs refer to others as "brother", you understand that in order to be a true "Brother", you must be in God's family by knowing Jesus as your Savior.

Spend the time learning what others believe. Do not be afraid! If you truly trust the Lord, your faith will not be shaken, but in fact, strengthened. The Holy Spirit will be there to ensure you do not become deceived. The more you know what is false, while also learning the truth, the more you will see clearly how everything outside of true Christianity is false.

There are many sources out there to help you understand other faiths. There is a list at the back of this book at which you can look. I would start with what J.S.M. offers.

If you are hungry to learn about the religions of the world to be a better servant and minister of the truth, God will provide for you. He owns all, so there is nothing He cannot provide those who desire to serve Him.

The Apostle Paul was not a man whose eyes were set on what the world had to offer. He compared the riches of the world and its fame to garbage after he came to know Jesus. Paul said, ***"I have learned, in whatever state I am, therewith to be content."* (Philippians 4:1)** His focus was on doing God's work. Here was a man who could have had all the world offered if he would have only stayed in his "religion". However, he traveled the known world, preaching the Gospel of Jesus Christ, fixing tents to make money to live, having next to nothing of his own except his clothes, his scrolls, and his faith, and told all who would listen, ***"But my God shall supply all your need according to His riches in glory by Christ Jesus"* (Philippians 4:19).** Now that is trusting in the Lord!

Dealing With Other Faith Groups

As in the free world, prison is filled with people of various faiths. However, in prison, much of your time is spent around men who do not share your faith because you are placed in the same prison, unit (cell block), and even cell. Learning to interact with these men is crucial. How can you share the Gospel with someone if you do not interact with him? Remember, these men are not your enemy. They may not believe what you believe, but that does not mean your battle is with them. The Lord tells you through Paul, that your battle is not with flesh and blood **(see Ephesians 6:12-18)**. The battle is a spiritual battle. That is why he instructed you to *"fight the good fight of faith"* **(1 Timothy 6:12)**.

As a young Christian in prison I learned the hard way that you can never win people to the Lord by "rubbing their faces" in how wrong they are. People are emotionally tied to their beliefs. You must respect the fact that they have a belief, though you may not agree with it.

What you will find is that all religions have some very specific things in common: they are all based upon works, and they all try to disprove Christianity and/or the Bible. Why? Because this is Satan's aim. All he has to do is place doubt in someone's mind, and he wins. The religions of the world are very cunning, and usually very subtle in doing this, so you need to be aware of the fact that this is their goal. Do not be surprised. Do not be alarmed. The battle is not yours. Here is what God says to us:

"Thus saith the Lord unto you, Be not afraid nor dismayed by reason of this great multitude; for the battle is not yours, but God's (2 Chronicles:20:15)

If God tells us not to be upset about even a great multitude against us, then we have no reason to be bothered about some unbelievers and scoffers. Remember this: the moment you become upset because of what someone believes or says, you begin, right then and there, to push them away from the truth. When you hear others tell of what they believe, even as crazy and offensive as it may be at times, it is only God giving you an opportunity to see where they are so you can potentially meet them at their point of need. In other words, you can use the opportunity to lead the person to the truth by helping them understand that their belief(s) is false. Let us be clear on this: outside the Gospel of Jesus Christ and Him Crucified, everything is false!

Use your conversations with other people to motivate you to dig more deeply into the Word of God. Do not just recognize that they believe something false, be able to gently and humbly explain to them the reason for your faith.

What I have found is that the deeper someone is into their "religion", the tougher it is to get them to see the truth. That does not mean it is impossible, but means you have to work at it in different ways. For instance, since you know that **"people do not care what you know until they know that you care",** building a relationship with them is going to be essential. If the extent of your relationship with someone from a different belief is only showing him where he is wrong, he is going to begin to avoid you pretty quickly! Remember, your job is not to prove him wrong, but to lead him to the truth through love.

You will find that, from time to time, people of other faiths will try to antagonize you, sometimes more than just "from time to time". Get used to it; this is what the world does. If you let your pride show its ugly head, you lose. It is that simple. This is why holding your peace, at times, and choosing your battles with others carefully is the key. You are not called to defend God. He is rather capable on His own. Your job is to share the truth in love. **(Ephesians 4:15)**

Let us look at the reality of your responsibility and the condition of the lost. If you do not take the time to reach-out to them with the truth, who will? It is you whom God has placed where you are to do this. You could be in many other prisons, or even dead, but God spared you. He desires to use you. Your mission field is where you are. You need to spend your time familiarizing yourself with your own belief very well; learning what they believe, also; developing your skills at sharing the truth; and winning them to Christ.

As I said previously, people neither like to relinquish/yield their beliefs very easily, nor admit that they have been wrong. Their pride tells them they cannot be wrong! When people have much invested in something, like their religion, their pride tells them they must not be wrong because they would then be forced to admit it. That would be a shame and embarrassment, which they will want to avoid at all costs. Blinded by pride, religious men will defend what they claim to believe even until death many times. Religious pride is the most blinding and destructive of all! You can never expect good results from butting heads with people of other faiths. How do I know all this? I have made every mistake that one can make in this area. I had to learn, after many apologies and times feeling like an idiot, that I needed to check myself and my motives before engaging in dialogue with others. I learned that I could not allow their bad attitudes toward the Bible, Christianity, Jesus, and other Brothers, or myself to affect how I dealt with them. I remember one time a guy I know had a book which claimed to expose Christianity, called "The Greatest Story Ever Sold!" I was really hurt by what it said. I knew the claims were lies. However, trying to "defend" Christianity after seeing that book would only have caused a disagreement. These lies were what he wanted to believe at the time. The best thing for me to do was simply recognize his predicament, and then begin to extend kindness to him. Remember, love never fails, but pride does every time.

When you are able to see past the belief that the person professes, and begin to view him as a candidate for the Kingdom of God, your job becomes a whole lot easier. Understand: everyone in the world believes something. It may not be one of the popular religions, but everyone has a belief about whether or not there is a God, and where they will spend eternity. Since most of the people you contact do not know the truth (Yes I said most!), that means that almost everyone you see and meet has a different faith. Stop going through life as though God has personally commissioned you to tell others how wrong they are in their beliefs; humble yourself and lead them to the truth: Jesus Christ, and Him Crucified.

Church Business: Being Wise—it's Private!

Nothing fuels the fires of Christian slander more than unbelievers and even young, immature Believers hearing or overhearing Brothers talk about problems in the Body. Countless times I have seen and heard Brothers openly talking about these things while others are listening to their conversations. The damage this causes is immeasurable and avoidable. All it does is reinforce in people's minds that they do not want to be a part of what they perceive as being the Church! For young Believers who are too immature to understand what is taking place, it sets a terrible example and leads them to believe that this type of behavior is acceptable. Be advised: young Believers rarely have enough sense not to take what they hear and then go tell other people. They are still babes and they do fleshly things. Just like parents need to never argue in front of their children; those who have been walking with the Lord faithfully for a while should know never to discuss church business with those who are not ready to handle such things.

Let me "break this down" even further so you can understand clearly: never talk about problems that arise within the Body of Christ when an unbeliever is present. **NEVER!!** You need to be aware of your surroundings at all times, whether in the unit, the rec. yard, the chapel, the chow hall or anywhere else. Those people close by, who look as if they are doing something besides listening to you: those are the very ones who listen to what you are saying and take all they hear and use it to slander you and the Body of Christ. Make no mistake: the very ones who try to do this usually are the ones who call themselves

"Christians". Most of your opposition will come from those who "profess" Christ.

Even further, NEVER share information about problems within the Body with immature Believers. You will cause severe damage. It will bite you.

There are going to be times problems arise within the Body, which is only normal. If you are doing your best to stand for the truth—the Message of the Cross—the Gospel—you will become the target of the forces of evil, and they will use many people—mostly in the Church—to cause problems. The last thing you need when trying to do right and help to solve problems/bring peace, is for your thoughts and plans to be blabbed to someone who is working out of the flesh so he can sabotage what you are doing. Church business needs to be kept among those who are directly involved, and even then, you must use wisdom (discretion, prudence, discernment, subtlety).

As well, as a minister and leader/counselor, there will be times when men come to you and confide very personal information. Some will confess their struggles with sin. Some will reveal that they have been convicted of a sexual offense. Others will tell you that they have testified against someone. Whatever the case, I warn you very sternly: do not ever betray this trust by sharing this information with others, nor treat them differently than any other Brother! You NEVER expose another Brother's weakness or flaw. And do not be fooled by your own pride and conceit. If not for the grace of God, you would be involved in and guilty of the worst sin imaginable, including nailing the Lord to the Cross! This means that the moment you look down upon the homosexual, the child molester, the assaulter of the elderly, etc., you have forgotten who you really are: a wretched sinner whom Christ has saved.

Paul said, *"And do you think this, O man, who judges them which do such things, and do the same, that you shall escape the Judgment of God?"*

Or despise you the riches of His goodness and forbearance and longsuffering; knowing that the goodness of God leads you to repentance?" (Romans 2:3-4)

The Bible says, *"Let not your good be evil spoken of."* **(Romans 14:16)**

When unbelievers and immature Believers hear things they should not hear, or for which they are unready, your words can EASILY be turned against you, and they will. This is unprofitable to the ministry, and is avoidable. Do right; instruct others to do the same; immediately do your best to stop this when you see it begin to happen, and you will save yourself much trouble and heartache. If a Brother is all "worked-up" and you cannot get him to exhibit self-control over his tongue regarding an issue, then try your best to walk him to an area where no one can hear him. Bring him in your cell if you have to. Be gentle and kind, and usually he will listen.

Be wise! Everyone is Listening!

Interaction with Guards and Those in Authority

One of the most common occurrences in prison is to hear someone complain about a guard, a counselor, a case manager, a warden, or any other staff member. Most do not understand that these people are not their enemies. The mindset is usually that they are in prison because someone told on them, the police and prosecutor were wrong in arresting and convicting them, and that their latest enemy, the prison staff, is holding them captive. Few realize or admit that it was THEIR SIN that brought them to prison, and that God orchestrated it all through their bad choices.

We know that we do not live in a perfect world and that even those who are supposed to uphold the law, in fact, take the law into their own hands and break it. But this neither excuses nor gives license to the ones incarcerated to disrespect authority.

The Word says, *"Let every soul be subject unto the higher powers. For there is no power but of God: the powers that be are ordained of God.*

Whosoever resisteth the power resisteth the ordinance of God: and they that resisteth shall receive to themselves damnation.

For rulers are not a terror to good works, but to the evil. Wilt thou then not be afraid of the power? Do that which is good, and thou shalt have the praise of the same.

For he is the minister of God to you for good. But if you do that which is evil, be afraid; for he bears not the sword in vain: for he is the minister of God, a revenger to execute wrath upon him who does evil." **(Romans 13:1-4)**

Let me make my point very clear: I am not saying that as Christians we are to blindly follow every man-made law and rule that government makes. If man's law goes against what God says in His Word, then we are to obey the Higher Authority, God. However, this is rarely the case in prison, although it does happen. This is why Paul proceeded to say, *"Wherefore you must needs be subject, not only for wrath, but also for conscience sake."* **(Romans 13:5).** When you are told to break God's law, you do not fear the wrath of man, you obey your conscience (what you know to be right) and do as God says, regardless of the consequences/penalties involved.

The text is very plain: it is the Lord who puts people into positions of authority. When you rebel against the law and those who uphold them, you are in fact rebelling against the Lord. Even further, when you complain about these people you are speaking evil of them. Paul instructed Titus to *"Put them in mind to be subject to the principalities and powers, to obey magistrates, to be ready to every good work,*

"To speak evil of no man, to be no brawlers, but gentle, showing all meekness unto all men." **(Titus 3:1-2).**

What you have to realize is this: The vast majority of people in authority in prisons are decent people trying only to do their jobs. Do they err at times? Of course they do. They are only human like you and I. Do some abuse their power?

Certainly, some do. The same goes for police and prosecutors. However, you must accept the fact that it is God who has allowed them to abuse that authority. He did not tell them to do so, nor does He approve of what they do. But as when God hardened Pharaoh's heart, the ruler of Egypt, to disobey God's command to let His people go, God will give these men courage to continue in their foolish ways because God knows what is really in their heart: the desire to do evil.

Since it is God who allows all this, what should your stance as a Believer in prison be? To begin, you need to check yourself to see whether or not you harbor any type of wrongful attitude towards those in authority, even ones who may have done you harm. If there is a problem—fix it. If you need to forgive --- do so. If you cannot humble yourself to do these things --- you will halt your forward progress and begin to backslide!

Next, you need to realize the example you set will have a major effect on your ministry to others. If people see you disgruntled with a staff member, or hear you complain about a prosecutor, they will either follow your lead, look at you as a hypocrite, or both. This leads only to trouble. If you trust that the Lord is in control, your emotions will stop going up and down like a yo-yo.

As you finally begin to understand this, you will see clearly that the ones in authority will become an asset to you, not some sort of foe. You need to realize that they are only people like you and I and that they respond the same way we do most of the time. If someone is rude or discourteous to you, how do you feel? Not very good right? The same goes for people in authority. When they are "talked down to", disrespected, laughed-at, yelled-at, etc., they feel the same type of emotions. How can you or I expect someone to look favorably upon us if we make them feel that way? You may have simply viewed them as "those on the other side", but they are just people who went a different way in life than you. Treat them kindly, and you will see how very quickly they will begin to treat you kindly. God will begin to give you favor with everyone around you when you deal with others as the Lord would have you do.

Let us look at the life of Joseph to see an example of a man who was right in God's eyes! Joseph resisted the temptation to lay with his master's wife, and for this he was thrown into prison like a real criminal. On top of that, years before, Joseph had been thrown in a pit by his own brothers, and then sold into slavery by strangers to strangers. If anyone had a reason to complain, would not it have been this man? But what did he do instead? He trusted the Lord. He took his eyes off his circumstances and had faith that God was in control, both of all that transpired, plus his future. Immediately he began to be blessed with the favor of God by being bought by Potiphar. This man, Potiphar, trusted Joseph, a Hebrew slave, with all that he had. And although the evil of Potiphar's wife caused Joseph a major problem, he did not stop trusting in the Lord. Did God have a plan for his life? Yes, He did. Did Joseph see that plan in its entirety? No he did not. But he still trusted the Lord. Did he complain and carry-on after he was thrown into prison, blaming Potiphar's wife, his own brothers from years before, or even God? No, he humbled himself. What happened? The Word says, ***"The Lord was with Joseph, and showed him*** *mercy and gave him favor in the sight of the keeper of the prison.*

"And the keeper of the prison committed to Joseph's hand, all the prisoners that were in the prison; and whatsoever they did there, he was the doer of it.

"The keeper of the prison looked not to anything that was under his hand; because the Lord was with him, and that which he did, the Lord made it to prosper. **(Genesis 39:21-23).**

If God gave so much favor to Joseph, a mere man like you and me, He will do the same for anyone who is willing to trust Him. Will it be the same exact way? Perhaps not, but you can be secure knowing that it will be in the *best* way. It always is when you do it His way.

You have to understand, also, that there are staff members who are Christians, as well. When they see your character as a Believer who loves the Lord, they will respect that. In fact, some of the greatest honors bestowed upon me in prison have been when a staff member—including wardens— have stopped me and said, "please pray for my son, daughter, loved one, etc.". If you are real, and you trust in the Lord fully, you will begin to see these things happen in your ministry. Do not be afraid of what others will say. They are going to talk about you anyway! Truth be told, those who have something to say about the favor the staff will give you only wish that they were able to receive the same, but they know that their attitude, communication, and character are badly flawed. That is okay; be kind to them regardless.

Here is what I have experienced: It does not matter where you are; if one man begins to "stand-up" and do right, others will follow. If one courageous leader stands for the truth, he will draw others. What was once uncommon becomes the norm. However, this takes determination and guts. You cannot be concerned about what others say as you treat the staff with respect. Do what you know to be what the Lord would have you to do.

In your personal prayer life, pray for those in authority. Pray that God would give them wisdom to carry-out their duties. Pray the Lord would draw them closer, and that they would see the Lord's Hand working, and be more grateful, thereby helping the men out who do right.

The Apostle Peter said to us, *"Submit yourselves to every ordinance of man for the Lord's sake: whether it be to the king, as supreme:*

"Or unto Governors, as unto them that are sent by him for punishment of evildoers, and for the praise of them who do well.

"For so is the will of God, that with well doing you may put to silence the ignorance of foolish men:" (1 Peter 2:13-15).

I do warn you sternly, however!: *"Give none occasion to the adversary to speak reproachfully"* (1 Timothy 5:14). As well, *"give no offense in anything, that the ministry be not blamed:* (1Corinthians 6:13).

If you do not use wisdom in your dealings with staff members, you will quickly open the door for gossip and slander to begin. What you mean for good will be taken and used against you, as the enemy always seeks to do. Your testimony is what Satan will target, while he is attacking your faith. So what you ought to do is make sure that your dealings with the staff are as open as possible. If need be, bring someone with you when you speak to them about various issues. Keep the length of your conversations brief. As time goes on and you deal with the staff more and more, this will be important. People in prison start to mistrust someone who is always talking to a staff member, so you need to make sure that you are not perceived negatively. Is that fair? No, but "fair" is irrelevant. Your goal is to be effective. Does that mean that you have to be very short in your conversations always with the staff? No, but always be mindful of the enemy turning your good efforts into looking as if you are the "bad guy". And because of the fear of politics in prison, once people begin to chatter and gossip about you, it is difficult for others to open up to you. They may even like you, but because of being fearful of what others may say, they keep to themselves and you lose the chance to minister. All this can be avoided by your using wisdom.

I have discovered: once you have established yourself as a man of God, you will be given some lee-way in this area because people know who you are and what you are about. They trust and see that your being a Christian does not mean you are the prison tattle-tale. However, new people are always coming into prison so you must not take for granted the fact that since many know you, you can throw caution to the side.

Dealing with staff in a respectful, Godly way will be of tremendous importance and blessing to you in your ministry and overall time in prison. Humble yourself and use wisdom.

One last note: Inmates in prison, feeling that they are never wrong and that the staff always is, are quick to file complaints against prison officials, including chaplains. Many times this gets quick results. However, we are not the general public, and filing a grievance against a staff member, especially a chaplain, is the very last resort that any Christian should ever take, particularly if the staff member is a real Brother or Sister in Christ. Paul forbids Christians to take each other for judgment before unbelievers. **(See 1 Corinthians 6:1-7)** We do not deal with problems as the world does, in particular when being persecuted because of our faith. We are called to use our sufferings as opportunities to praise and glorify the Lord, not moan and complain as the unsaved. If the chaplains discriminate against you; praise God that you are counted worthy to suffer for His name's sake. Do not write them up as the other faith groups do. Understand that God either causes or allows everything in life to happen. Do not be shocked or alarmed when you are mistreated by staff, or your "rights" are taken away, including chapel time slots, Bible studies, materials, etc. Trust the Lord that He is in control, and your life will be a lot easier.

Dealing with Other Races

The prison population consists of all races of people. Your ministry is certainly not limited to your own race and skin color, so you have to be able to effectively deal with people who are not of the same race as yourself.

To begin with, let us be very clear; the Word says that God is no respecter of persons, and neither are we to be **(See Romans 2:11)**. If you have any objections about dealing with other races, you had better repent. If you show favoritism toward a particular race, such as your own, it will be very evident sooner or later. You are only fooling yourself if there is some sort of bias or prejudice in your mind that you have not settled. Christ died for everyone, and in God's eyes, we are all the same. But are we not all a mix of different colors, nationalities, countries, and cultures? How can we then be the same? Because, even though there are outward differences, God looks at the heart. And how are we the same there? The Word tells us that our hearts—every single one of us---are *"deceitful above all things and desperately wicked"* **(Jeremiah 17:9)**. So if you think that you are somehow better than someone who is different than you, you had best reconsider. You are not. You may have been regenerated, but you began as wickedly as everyone else.

Read what Paul says in **1 Corinthians 4:6-7,** *"And these things, Brethen, I have in a figure transferred to myself and to Apollos for your sakes; that you might learn in us not to think of men above that which is written, that no one of you be puffed up for one against another V7. "For who makes you to* *differ from another? and what have you that you did not receive? now if you did receive it, why do you glory, as if you had not received it?*

When dealing with other races you need to become familiar with their backgrounds and cultures. Talk to them. Learn what they have experienced in life. Allow them to share with you what they most value, or what has hurt them the worst. Discover what type of prejudice they have faced. Make an effort to know them! Even if you see that someone is closed off to the Gospel, you can still benefit from listening to their stories as you witness to others of similar backgrounds. If you will venture into this area you will begin to see a wider harvest of souls come to the Lord.

In today's prisons we find a very large population of Spanish-speaking men. Your ministry need not be only to those of your own country. I have found that one of the best blessings in my ministry, so far, has been helping men from Mexico and other Spanish speaking countries learn the Message of the Cross, and not only to see their lives begin to change before my eyes, but to help prepare them to take back to their countries what has changed their lives. Can you begin to see the opportunity here? Your poor choices got you into prison, but God, in His abundant love and mercy, has opened a spiritual door for you to be able to be a part of His great harvest of souls from right where you are! The work that you do will have an effect on people in foreign countries! Is that awesome, or what? We have a mighty, forgiving, gracious God.

J.S.M. now has the Expositor's Study Bible available in Spanish, which contains the Old and New Testaments. Those of us who have a ministry to the Spanish-speaking people have waited eagerly for the completion of this wonderful tool. As well, J.S.M. has other products available and being completed in Spanish, now. These will be invaluable to the men in your ministry.

Since you have a ministry to the Spanish-speaking people around you, I suggest that you learn Spanish yourself, if you have not done so already. Not only will it be helpful to communicate, but you will see that you will begin to gain a level of respect from these men that you have not experienced previously. Their hearts will be touched by the fact that you took the time to learn their language. This translates into your caring about them; therefore, they will be more open to the Gospel and being discipled afterward. Take advantage of this amazing opportunity. If you are serious about your ministry (if you are close to God and His love compels you), reach everyone with whom you come in contact.

Being effective in your ministry to other races can be a challenge at times; not because there is no desire to do so, but because of background and cultural differences which you need to overcome. This is where the "Being Real" part is so key. No one expects you to be perfect, and they will accept your differences, but they must see that you are genuinely concerned. You may not have come from the same economic background as they have — perhaps you were fairly poor and they well-off, or the reverse — but if they can relate to you as a person — if you can help them to respect your character — then you will go far in helping them to open-up and hear the Gospel of Jesus Christ. Is that not what it is really about?

The Person in the Cell with You

Whether you call this person a "cellie", "bunkie", "cellmate", etc., it all means the same thing: the person with whom you share a cell. This relationship in prison is one that needs to be beneficial to both parties, in order for it to work. Many times you will see a Christian in a room with an unbeliever. This is common. What is also common is tension on both sides. The Christian complains about how worldly and disrespectful his cellie is, and the unbeliever complains how..... worldly and disrespectful the Christian is! This should not be the case! For starters: you, as a Christian, need to learn one of the most important lessons in prison, which someone had to help me learn. It was told to me like this: "Let them do them!" It means that we are *never* to try to control other people. Also, *never* put expectations on these men. All you will do is be disappointed. You cannot expect the world to act any differently than the world does. If you are constantly being bothered or upset because your cellie does not do as you think he should, you have begun to put expectations on him. That is not your job. Your job is to be humble, reach-out in genuine love and care, and let your life be a testimony to what Christ has done in you. The way they will understand this is not through your many religious words, but through your life. Your cellie should say nothing short of, "I have the best cellie I've ever had". This only happens when you get out of the picture, and let the Holy Spirit work in you. "Self" has to die!

You must understand: cellies do not sin against us, but God. You really must stop taking all he does as though he were purposely doing something against you. As well, your relationship is not a "tit-for-tat" or some type of competition between you. Drop all the nonsense and humble yourself. If you cannot be loving and kind to a cellie, you will never treat your wife in a way that pleases God. Regardless of how offensive your cellie can be, your job is to forgive him, no questions asked! The easiest way to do this is to make a decision to forgive your cellie in advance, for all he will ever do. Then simply remind yourself (your pride) of this as your cellie lives his life and does things that you consider offensive. If you get to the point where you feel like things are not fair, and that you have become his servant—good! You are on the right track!

The Lord told a story in **Matthew 18:21-35** that you need to read a few times. A man, forgiven for over four billion dollars (today's worth in gold), refused to forgive a man who owed him about three hundred dollars. When the man who forgave the four billion dollar debt heard that the man he forgave would not forgive another man, he had him locked-up in prison until he paid his original debt of four billion dollars. What God is saying here is that when we do not forgive others for the things they do to us (much of it even being unintentional), such as what cellies do, we are really telling the Lord that we could not care less what He has forgiven us. Is this what you want?

Years ago I was in a cell with an old guy with whom I was not getting along. At first we did okay, but soon after I began to be offended over many things he did, while he claimed to be a Christian. It got so bad that I did not even wish to speak to or be around him, and I tried to work my schedule so we were in the cell together as little as possible. Things got to the point that I could not even stand to hear his voice. I began to despise him.

Each day I would get up in the morning before he awoke and would go to the rec. yard to run. I had to, at that point, because I found myself so angry being in the cell with him. I felt as though he were driving me crazy. I was irritable much of the time, and I had no peace or joy. I was praying to get out of the cell, but there were no others available for months. When I would run each day, I would lose most of that anger. The exercise really calmed me. If I did not run and deplete my energy I was like a bear robbed of her cubs.

One day I went out to the yard and ran around the track. I was listening to a Christian radio station, as I did most mornings. The preacher said to the listeners, "Is there someone in your life who makes you angry?" Immediately I got excited and said to myself, "This is what I have been waiting for!" The preacher went on to say, "Does this person drive you crazy when you are around him?" I said to myself, "Yes!! the Lord is speaking to me!" The preacher said, "Does the sound of this person's voice disgust you?" I said, "Thank you Lord, yes!!", waiting for the Lord to tell me how to fix my cellie. The preacher then said, "Do you just want to give this person a piece of your mind each time you see him?" I practically screamed out loud, "Yes, yes, yes!!!" And then the preacher dropped the bomb: *"You have a problem with pride"*, he said, and my heart sank as I cried, "No, not me!"

God gave me insight to my problem that day, and it was not my cellie, but my own foolish pride. You see, even though my cellie had issues, God was showing me what was so ugly inside of myself, not him. I could not see that before that time because I was blinded by my own pride and self-righteousness. The entire time I was pointing my finger at his faults and complaining about all he had done to offend me, I was in reality that man in the parable who would not forgive the small debt that someone had incurred with me. All I could think about was myself, my convenience, my comfort, etc. It was a very tough, humiliating lesson to learn. I pray you will learn from my mistakes.

When you do right, you stop all your complaining because your focus is on the Lord, not what your cellie did or did not do. As well, your cellie will stop complaining about you because you become a delight with which to live, not a fault-finding "religious person" who makes him feel like you think of him as inadequate. Some of my bitterest moments in prison have been because of the situations with my cellies. I had to realize that even though the person with whom I was in the cell had problems, the real fault was in me and my pride. God allowed me to see through those situations how horrible I really was inside, all the while blaming the other person.

The cellies you will have in prison will be used by the Lord to teach you. The Lord is going to use them to mold and shape you as you go, *if* you are willing to humble yourself and take full responsibility for the relationship. In other words, no matter how things get between you, you must *always* be willing to look at yourself and say, "What could I have done better? Stay away from blaming whatever happens on that person (or anyone for that matter!), and begin to look at why God allowed these things to happen. Many times over the years I have heard people say that they were in a cell with someone because their cellie needed to be shown something from them. All they could see was what that person lacked, and how "God was going to use them" to show their cellie the "truth". The reality is, many Believers are too blind spiritually to see that God is using the unbeliever to wake up the Believer to where he falters. You may have a tendency to run around thinking that you are this spiritual giant, and that God has anointed you to change the world. Wrong! You are simply a Believer who is in need of much growth. God uses those around you to bring-out in you the things that need to be surrendered to Him, completely.

Your cellie should be a walking advertisement of how you, with your faults and all, love the Lord and care for the people of this world, starting with him. If you cannot humble yourself to make that happen, you are in for a long, rough road. Even further, people around you are going to judge you and your walk by how well you get along with your cellie. If there are always problems, that will be a bad reflection upon you. If you have a cellie that has many problems, do your best to be the best friend you can be while you are with him. Set the best example that you can. The person in the cell with you will benefit from it, others will learn from your example, and God will bless you.

One last word on cellies: many problems can be eliminated by your making sure that you clean the cell often, *without* putting any expectation on him to do the same. If you will do it "unto the Lord" as you are supposed to do everything, you will never be disappointed. Your motive is never to be that your cellie appreciates what you have done. He will not many times! It must be to please the Lord, Who will always appreciate your faith inspired obedience, and who will take care of you.

Personal Fitness and Hygiene

I once knew a man who loved the Lord and tried his best to witness to others, but his breath was so bad that no one wanted to stand close to him. Your ministry has to be a complete package. If you have body odor, bad breath, sloppy eating habits, poor grooming, or a messy appearance, you will do more to turn people away from the Gospel then draw them to the Lord Whom you say you serve. If you are in poor physical shape because of bad eating habits and no exercise, you are not putting your best foot forward. I realize that these things have little to do with the actual Gospel, but you must remember you are working with the lost and very immature Believers. What they see before them will have an effect on them one way or another. You do not want something for which you are responsible to be the stumbling block for someone to whom you are witnessing. Do your best to glorify the Lord in all you do, and that means in your appearance and personal hygiene, as well. It makes a difference, and if you want to be the best you can be in your ministry, you will pay attention to this area.

The following is a list of personal responsibilities that may seem elementary, common knowledge, but all too often people fail to keep them.

- Brush your teeth 2-3 times per day. NEVER leave the cell in the morning without brushing your teeth and drinking a glass of water right after. Morning acid in your stomach gives you bad breath, also.

- Scrape/brush your tongue with toothpaste *every* time you brush your teeth. Bacteria will stick to your tongue, causing bad breath and ugliness.

- Floss daily. Food caught between your teeth stinks.

- Clean your ears thoroughly.

- Clean the sand out of your eyes in the morning before you walk out of your cell.

- Cut your fingernails and toenails.

- Clean your fingernails often.

- Shower daily (multiple times if needed)

- Use deodorant

- Do not bite your nails.

- Use clean clothing daily (do not reuse socks, underwear, t-shirts, etc.)

- Groom yourself (cut nose hair, ear hair, etc.)

- Look presentable at all times.

- Change your linens often (at least once a week)

- Blow your nose when you have to! Do not snort and suck on your snot around others ever, but especially at the table or when it is quiet.

- Cover your face when you sneeze, but not with the hand which you will shake people's hands afterward. Wash your hands after you sneeze! (Cough or sneeze into the inside of your elbow, so you can clean it later.)

The object here is not to be vain or conceited, but to make a positive impression as an ambassador of Christ here on earth.

Commissary Items and Medicine

Part of the ministry is the privilege of meeting the physical needs of those around you at times while you help them spiritually. Since all you have belongs to the Lord anyway, you need to use what you have in ministry. What is a soul's worth to you? Is it not worth even your last dollar? There are times when you will be able to use soups, coffee, creamer, Tylenol, allergy tabs, cough syrup, etc. to be a blessing to people. This is an excellent way to build your relationship with them. Is it bribing them? Call it what you will—and I have been accused of it all!—but I could not care less what people say; if the giving of these items gives us an opportunity to share with people the Gospel, so be it! Use whatever you need to use as long as it does not bring shame to the Gospel.

I have had some of the best success in my ministry through sharing with others some inexpensive commissary items. You need to understand that since very, very few people in prison really share freely with others what they have, you will really touch the hearts of many by doing so. Since people naturally feel gratitude and a debt to those who give to them, they are that much more inclined to either hear your testimony, be invited and commit to going to a Bible Study, or even hear the Message of the Cross, repent, and give their lives to the Lord, all because you gave them something to eat or for their headache, etc.

Let me ask you this: Do you really think any material item you have will matter the day you stand before the Lord? What will? Only what you did for Him (out of faith, love, and obedience!) So be prepared when they come to you in need (not simply want!). It will not cost you much, but it can and will pay you eternal dividends if you use what you have wisely.

Telling Others That You Love Them

Prison is filled with men walking around with their chests puffed-out to convince each other how tough they are. Most feel that if they were to show their emotions, such as joy, gratitude, humility, or love, it would be taken as a sign of weakness on their part. They spend their time faking and hiding their emotions, trying to look "cool". They try to uphold their "image" at all costs.

The truth is, the same emotions people on the outside of prison experience, those in prison do also. Most men in prison are simply too *afraid* to let others see what they are really feeling inside.

My very first week in prison, which was in no ordinary prison but a Federal Penitentiary, which holds the men that society calls the worst criminals (the only higher level security prison is a "Super-Max", which holds those that cannot interact with other prisoners,) I had a learning-lesson that has forever stuck with me and made a big difference in my walk with the Lord in prison. One day I was walking back to my unit, and I saw a guy heading towards me. I did not recognize him at first because I was brand-new, and I was seeing so many new faces. As he drew closer, he called out to me: "Brother Russell", and I quickly realized that I had met him at the daily prayer group which had meetings at the chapel each day. I had been introduced to him only once, and it had been two or three days earlier.

You have to picture the scene in order to appreciate what took place. Here I was, walking on the sidewalk alone, except for this man approaching me from the opposite direction. To the sides of us were men gathered together, hanging-out, just passing the time watching (scoping!) all that went on around them, and listening. They were all the tough-looking characters. Here comes this man towards me calling my name, and he was 6'3"-6'4", black and weighed 260-270. Here I am, 5'8", white, and obviously much smaller. The Brother extends his hand to me and says, "Are you good, Brother Russell—do you need anything?" to which I said "Thanks, but I think that I am all set-up". He then tells me, "O.K., I'll see you tonight at the prayer-group", and we shook hands and said goodbye. I started back walking to my unit, and I could see these guys to the sides of me checking-out who I was. I could feel their eyes on me as I walked. I had gotten about twenty feet from where I had said goodbye to the Brother, when all of a sudden I heard the Brother yell out, "Oh Brother Russell", and when I turned around to look at him he said, "I love you, Brother". I almost fainted! Here I was at a USP, in the middle of the day, with guys everywhere hearing what was being said, and this man yells out to me, "I love you"! I did not know what to do. I mumbled something back like, "Thanks, Bro" and headed back to my unit. God was trying to show me something, but my pride had me in a whirlwind. I, too, just like most of the prison, was still worried about my "image", and what others would think. Here was a man whom I barely knew, but who sincerely cared about me as a Brother enough to put himself out there that way. What an amazing lesson I learned once I grew-up a bit and put my foolish pride to the side. NEVER be embarrassed or ashamed to tell someone that you love him. Who cares what others think! In fact, many wish they could say the same to someone else, but they cower to their fears. From that one incident God taught me a huge lesson that I have carried with me all my years in prison and it has had an impact on not just me, but many others as well. Once you "break the ice" by saying this to people, and they know that you are sincere, it becomes a part of your relationship with them. When you say it, though, you had better mean what you say. When you look people in the eyes they will know whether or not you truly love them. As well, letting a Brother (or anyone else) know that you love him means there is no more room for walking around pretending to be the "tough guy" that no one actually is. Do not misunderstand what I am saying: I do believe that the toughest men in prison, who walk the toughest walk, are sold-out for the Lord, Christians. But that is a much different "tough guy" than what the world perceives as being tough.

Do not be afraid or ashamed to tell someone that you sincerely love him and care about him. You will make a difference in his life. Most people in prison need to know, even though they are separated from their relatives, they are still loved and valued by others. Do not let your pride get in the way of making a difference in someone's life around you.

Humor and its Boundaries

Everyone enjoys a good laugh, and the Word tells us, *"A merry heart makes a cheerful countenance: but by sorrow of the heart the spirit is broken"* **(Proverbs 15:13)**

As Christians, much of the time we do not rejoice enough. We have a natural (fallen) tendency to focus on the problems, not our solution, Jesus. Having good, clean fun is a necessity in our lives, and surely is one of the benefits of our dedicated service. Some of my best times in prison have been laughing with the Brothers over situations or at our own stupidity and foolishness. We need to be able to look at ourselves and be joyous after we have learned important lessons. Many times we will simply shake our heads and say with a smile, "How could I have been so blind?" Likewise, there are a lot of times to jump for joy when we experience a victory over the enemy, which includes using some humor.

I would say this, however: always be careful how far you take your humor. As in every other decision, be wise. Do not allow a funny thought to be a stumbling block to someone else, or even further, something you have to go back and apologize for doing or saying.

The humor in which you are involved must always be appropriate. Our ways and thoughts are not to be the same as the world's, so tasteless, coarse "joking" is never acceptable.

Here is what Paul said, *"but fornication, and all uncleanness, or covetousness, let it not be not once named among you , as becomes Saints; "Neither filthiness, nor foolish talking, nor jesting, which are not convenient: but rather giving of thanks"* **(Ephesians 5:3-4).**

Paul put inappropriate humor in the same category as fornication, uncleanness, covetousness, etc. That only tells us how serious God looks at this. It can only harm your testimony and witness to others.

On the flip-side of things, as a Christian you are going to hear much of this nonsense at times. How are you to react to the telling of filthy jokes, or simply inappropriate or vile humor? Firstly, you should rarely be around this type of situation. However, if it is unavoidable, like being at work, then simply go about your business. When unbelievers (or even those who claim to be Believers!) have vulgar or profane conversations, NEVER participate! Do not laugh at dirty or racially-charged jokes, or jokes which demean people, even staff, or other inmates even if they bring-on most of their own troubles. **(See Proverbs 14:9).** This is not to say that the jokes will not be funny at times, but the witness you have for the Gospel of Jesus Christ in your testimony must be valued much more highly than a couple of laughs. Always err on the side of caution when dealing with people's feelings. Remember, people will always remember you for how you made them feel.

"A Brother offended is harder to be won than a strong city: and their contentions are like the bars of a castle" **(Proverbs 18:19).**

When it comes to being around crude humor, you do not have to pretend you enjoy it, nor should you give others an attitude for being who they are: the lost. If you are taking it personally that these things are being said, you have a rough road ahead of you. Our job is not to judge the people of the world. If you are a Christian, they know you do not enjoy hearing such. Many times they just test you or "try you" to see what you will do. Let the world be the world! Treat them kindly no matter what. Do not try to make them feel bad or guilty for being who they are. Humble yourself and look for ways to share the Gospel with them. Handling things any other way puts you under a load that you are not to carry. Let the Lord do His job while you do yours.

Expectations

As I mentioned, putting expectations on people is a recipe for disaster. Surely you would like to see others do their best, and never falter, but it is very unrealistic to think that this will ever happen. Yes, there are some Brothers you will meet who can be trusted no matter what, but these are rare gems and not the norm. The reality is that all of us are a work-in-progress, and we all make mistakes and disappoint at times. If you understand this, it should be no surprise to you when it happens. It usually is, however. The important thing is not so much what happened, as how you react. If you are always expecting perfection out of others, you are going to be up and down emotionally. You have to realize that part of each person's growth is making mistakes, as well as doing things differently at times from others. You "set yourself up for failure" if you do not take this into consideration.

When someone falls-short, take it in stride. Remember, if it were not for the grace of God that would be you. Use the situation as an opportunity to minister to the person, not make him feel as though he really blew it. Encourage him if need be. If it is simply a matter of someone's not meeting up to "your standard", look at that as well, and see if you need to check yourself.

Putting unrealistic expectations on others will only cause you problems. Understand that, in ministry, your job is to help those who may be struggling in areas, and this means they need to have the confidence that you, a spiritual leader, are not going to reject them or "look-down on them" because they have fallen short. To the contrary, when someone has sinned/blundered, etc. you ought to be the one for whom they come looking, like Jesus is to us. Our ministry is not to condemn anyone. We are to love, heal, and forgive. We are to help people up, not kick them when they are down. Be assured, the tables will be turned at some point, and you will not want a "holier than thou" attitude from some pride-filled hypocrite, but a compassionate, humble Brother who understands that everyone stumbles.

One of the most common things I have experienced in this area is having someone tell me he was coming to a Bible Study or service, and not show up. Because of my love for the person, as well as how I know that what he missed would have been of great benefit to him, I have a tendency to want to feel "let-down". However, I had to realize a long time ago that this happens. Prison is not known for holding men who are the model of integrity, and who keep their word. That is okay. I have learned to simply treat them kindly and gently while saying things such as, "See if you can make it next week" when I see them. They know that they did not keep their word. There is no need to make an issue of it (most of the time!) and give them a lame excuse to never attend. That would be foolish to do. Treat them with love, and sooner or later, they will start coming to the studies and services. This principle holds true with all your dealings with others. If you make them feel bad, even when they failed to do as they said they would, you will never have an opportunity to accomplish what you really wish to do: win them to Jesus, and get them "on their feet" spiritually. Abandon the expectations and attitudes.

Evangelizing and Witnessing:

The word "Evangel" means "The Gospel", as defined by Webster's Dictionary. "Evangelize" means to "preach the Gospel", or "to convert". The Gospel Message is really the heart of your ministry. This Good News (The Gospel) is the answer to all of the age-old questions and the solution to all of the world's problems. What is this Good News? The Good News is that we can have a loving, healthy relationship with God as He intended, and which we so desperately need.

- Which age-old question does this answer? Who are we, and why are we here? We are creations of God, purposefully designed to have fellowship with Him. We are here to bring Him glory.

- What world problems are solved by this Good News? The root problem in this broken world is sin. Sin separates us from God, Who is Life, which brings about death, death in many forms. War, famine, disease, disasters, poverty, oppression, etc., are not the problems they seem to be, but are really symptoms of the true problem, which is sin. Although we combat the symptoms, there is nothing we as humans can do to cure sin. We are completely powerless against it. Even worse, sin does not just separate us from God, it makes us His enemies. The relationship can never be fixed from our own efforts.

Since we were all born in this condition, and have only made it worse in our misguided efforts to fix the problem, instead of turning to the Only One Who could, the fact that God has fully addressed these problems should come as *very* Good News.

It is God's will that each and every person on earth be given this Good News. God implemented a plan (discipleship) to make this happen, and equipped us to execute it (the Baptism of the Holy Spirit). That each and every person has not heard this plan does not reflect poorly on God, but indicts us, the sorry Church.

This is where you come into the picture. Someone directly, or indirectly, gave you the Good News, and Jesus has commissioned you to give it to others. Keep in mind, nothing good originates in you. It is the Holy Spirit Who fulfills this commission through your willingness and submission. You must allow Him to prepare you for the task. It is also He Who prepares the hearts of the potential converts to hear, understand, and accept the Gospel Message. If either of these preparations is not completed, then none of your witnessing techniques, talents, skills, smooth talking, etc., will produce any lasting tangible results. Your reliance must be on the Holy Spirit for every facet (part) of every step you take in witnessing, from the words you use, to the courage you need, to the people with whom you speak. You will need His leading and guidance to know whether the person needs to be convicted, or whether the person needs to be loved, etc. God tells us, *"Trust in the Lord with all your heart; and lean not on your own understanding. In all your ways acknowledge Him, and He shall direct your paths."* **(Proverbs 3:5-6)**

You will learn many effective approaches to sharing your faith, which are excellent to have at your disposal, but let the Holy Spirit lead you in which approach to take because only He knows the circumstances of that person's life, and what will affect them most powerfully.

There are many things that you need to learn to do effectively, and witnessing is one at which you need to become an expert. Aside from your life's being such that people around you will see Christ in all you do, learning how to lead people to Salvation is the next step. Do you have problems with communicating? So did Moses, but guess what? In trusting God he learned to overcome. If you are willing, God will make a way.

Over the years I have learned many things about effective Evangelizing and Witnessing. Much has been from trial and error. As you humble yourself to grow in God's grace, and as you learn more about His Word and about effectively interacting with people, you will be more comfortable sharing with others because you will be more confident in how to fully answer their questions. Many times you will not even have the time to answer people's question's because you may only be near them for a few minutes. This is why you need to learn specific techniques about how to help them see things from a spiritual perspective, which means that you are helping them see how lost they are and how they need a Savior desperately.

I recommend you start by getting a book by a Brother named Mark Cahill, called ONE THING YOU CAN'T DO IN HEAVEN. I have found this to be a dynamite book on witnessing. He will explain to you in very simple terms how to go about sharing your faith with others, effectively. Do not try to reinvent the wheel! Use techniques that have been proven to win souls to the Lord! Once you become more adept you can adjust what you say to fit your personal style so you can make the presentation your own. You should be relaxed and natural at this, which this book will help facilitate. Some prisons' libraries already have a copy of this book, so you may be able to find it where you are.

The use of "tracts", the little pamphlets or papers that are printed with the Gospel Message, can be very helpful to you, as well. You can share them with others and ask them what they think after they have read them. These tools really open the door for a one-on-one dialogue which can turn people to Christ. The best tracts that I have found thus far are available at Chick Publications, in California. They have a wide assortment which catches the attention of even the most seemingly uninterested observer.

There is no definitive answer to the question of when and where to witness to others. While there is never a set time or location, you will find that if you are willing, and you pray for the Lord to put you in front of those who need the Message of the Cross, He will. Remember, in order for someone to hear the Gospel and accept it, the Holy Spirit has to do the work. He must prepare the heart of that person, as well as prepare you if you are to be used. You need to allow Him to lead the way, and you must do this by diligently seeking His will and His leading before you are actually in the situation!

Anything short of this is simply a work of your flesh, and will produce very little of eternal value, if anything.

One of the biggest obstacles that people face when witnessing to others is their fear of being rejected (pride). I understand this is common, and I have experienced this fleshly fear, but it is irrelevant, and not to be regarded. Do not let a little bit of silly emotion damn someone's eternal soul and prevent you from accomplishing God's Will! Do not try to wiggle out of the fact that winning souls is *your* responsibility; it is not a "special calling" or "spiritual gift" for a select few.

When you look at the reality of this responsibility, you have to understand that you will come face to face with one of two persons; either the person before you, with whom you know you should be sharing your faith, or the Lord Himself one day, to Whom you will give an account of why you chose not to share (Read *Matthew 12:36).* So, by whom should we be concerned about being rejected, the lost sinner to whom God sent you, or God Himself? When you understand just how desperately all men need Salvation, you will be much less concerned over their reaction to your conversation about this subject. If folks do reject what you are saying, and even resent you for saying it, you should remember what the Lord said in **John 15:18:** *"If the world hate you , you know that it hated Me before it hated you".* You are in a battle and it is spiritual. Never lose sight of this. Do your best to share the truth with others, and disregard the consequences that seem so negative at times. Just make sure all your sharing is done in love.

I have found that once you condition your mind and heart to be looking for ways to share your faith with others, as well as the techniques to use, you will find that you will have many more interesting and profitable conversations than rejections, even with 'religious people", who are usually closed-off to the beliefs of others. You may not get them to denounce their man-made religion, but you will still plant or water a seed.

There is no short-cut to successfully sharing your faith. There are many tools you can use to educate yourself on evangelizing/witnessing, but to become proficient (well skilled) you must be actively engaged in soul wining on a regular/daily basis. The Word tells us that God will give us the desires of our heart if they are aligned with His will (see **Psalm 37:4**). If our desire is to be used as an effective witness to others, God will help us. The Word also tells us *"The fruit of the righteous is a tree of life; and he that wins souls is wise" (Proverbs 11:30)*

Where do you begin doing this? You begin by understanding that where you are is your mission field. Yes, you can expect God to send you people, or send you to them after you pray about it, but that should not deter you from actively seeking opportunities to share with others with whom you regularly come into contact. Begin your Gospel presentations by asking simple questions which will lead them to talk about their views on eternity and what they believe happens when someone dies. Most people will be eager to tell you their beliefs on this topic. Your job is not to "correct them", but to listen to them so you can get a better understanding of their beliefs and thoughts. Remember, no one likes to hear that they are wrong, so your job is to have a meaningful conversation that will get them to think about things about which they have never previously looked. Although there are some very intellectually dishonest people in prison, you will find that even most of these self-deceived, pseudo-intellectuals will at least "hear you out" and be honest when you present to them the truth. They may not make a decision for Christ right away, but you have gotten them to open their eyes to the fact that there are eternal things about which they need to think.

I believe you can be successful if you follow some simple basics: Pray first; show those around you that you are sincere and that you care about them; be well prepared to answer questions; be versed in your techniques that get others to talk about their beliefs on eternity; and let them see the joy and peace that the Lord has given you. These things, as well as trusting the Lord for the outcome, not you, will always yield fruit. You may not see it right away, but that is not the goal. The goal is to share the Message of the Cross, and to trust GOD for the increase after you plant and/or water seeds.

To recap: The goal is to trust God and share the Message of the Cross, understanding that increase may come down the road, and you may simply be planting the seed. All we are called to be is witnesses; not judges or juries!

Holding Bible Studies: Making Disciples

Bible studies are common in prison. Usually the chapel will offer one, and sometimes there are small groups that meet outside of the chapel, in the dorms or rec. yard. These can be good things, and can be very beneficial to those who attend, but be very, very clear on this point: if a Bible study is not centered on the Message of the Cross, you are only spinning your wheels. Unless someone understands that the Cross is the means which we receive everything good, not just for Salvation, then that person cannot properly understand the Bible, and will lead a very difficult Christian life. As I have heard it put so well on Brother Swaggart's program, "They will be miserably saved".

If the Bible Study that your prison offers is typical of most that I have seen so far in prison, then you need to seek the Lord about starting one of your own. If you do not yet understand the Message of the Cross—and most Christians *do not*—you must rearrange your priorities to do so. Otherwise you will be stumbling around the Bible, not knowing what to teach, giving your own interpretations of things. Get an **Expositor's Study**

Bible and begin to read all, both scripture and commentary.

Holding Bible studies is very simple. You, as the leader of the study, need to simply begin by praying and asking the Lord where He would have you start. It will usually be someplace with which everyone is familiar (at least with the name of a particular book), like the Gospels, and not a difficult book to understand for beginners, like Revelation or Daniel, etc. Let the Lord lead you.

Start by reading a few chapters ahead yourself, and then go back to the beginning. Go through, verse by verse, and be sure you can explain what the verse is saying. Next, on a notepad, write down in your own words what the verse means. Sometimes it will be that you will sum-up a few verses that go together, as well. When the study begins you can then refer to your notes and read them to help the others understand the text. Do not worry if you do not know the answer to every question. When you come across something of which you are unsure, simply tell them that you do not know but will find out the answer. People do not expect perfection, but they do expect you to be honest.

When you get the people together for the study, pick a time on which everyone can agree. Be willing to sacrifice on your end, if need be. There is nothing more important than this work. If they can only make it early in the morning, have it then. Late at night? Have it then. Be flexible. This is your calling and privilege.

When the group meets, pray at the outset and ask the Lord to prepare your hearts to receive. Then choose someone to read the verse with which you are starting. When he finishes the verse or section you tell him to read, then read your notes. Ask everyone if they understand. If they have any questions, they will ask you.

You must be mindful that *you* are the one leading the study, not anyone else. Always be kind and gentle, but do not allow someone to take control of the lead or to run away in conversation about things that do not relate to the subject you are studying. In other words, stay in control and on topic. You never want to come across as being domineering, but you do want to maintain the proper structure to accomplish your objective. If the conversation turns to other things, you simply say something along the line of , "O.K., let's get back to the study, so we can move on". As long as you do this lovingly but firmly, you will not have a problem. People at a Bible study are not there to hear what is for chow the next day, or the latest rumor on the compound. They want to learn. So if someone begins to take the conversation in a different direction, you simply guide it back on track.

Remember, Bible studies are not only about learning the particular text you are reading. They are about understanding the Bible, which is Jesus Christ, and Him Crucified. Once you begin to understand the Message of the Cross—the Gospel—you will then incorporate this into every study you hold because that is the whole purpose: to help others to see that their only hope and the source of all their blessings and victory, come to them by means of the Sacrifice at the Cross. The Bible studies I lead always, and without exception, point to the Cross. The men who do not yet understand this Message want to know more about it as they listen to someone (or many in the study!) tell them how they can have victory over sin, the world, and Satan. The men who have already experienced the power of the Cross want to know more about it because it brings them joy and strengthens their faith.

The purpose of the Bible Study is to help people understand the Bible so their lives can be changed by God's power, and so they can then share with others what God has done for them. Proper Bible studies make disciples of the Christians who attend. They are not about showing-off knowledge of the Bible that the leader has, but are about sharing the faith. As well, there can be others who attend who know the Message of the Cross, also, and these men can be of great help.

The way I structure our Bible studies is almost like a panel of people. One person leads and keeps structure, and the other men who have been attending for some time and know the Message of the Cross begin to add their own comments as we go. In other words, though everyone is encouraged to speak and ask questions, there are a select few who are on one accord with the aim of helping the younger Christians and candidates for Salvation to understand the Gospel in the text. It works very well so long as you have some men around you who are humble and surrendered to what you ought to achieve. Showboating has no place in this work.

In the beginning you may be the only one who understands (partially /theoretically) the Message. That will soon change, however, and as long as you are serious about your ministry, the Lord will place a few key individuals around you with whom you can share the Message (to others), and who will be a blessing to you and your ministry.

There are times when you will only get through a verse or two over the course of even a few hours, but that is not important. As long as you are covering the subject that you, as the leader, have been led by the Holy Spirit to cover, you are correctly teaching your Bible study.

Here is what needs to be covered in some way and to various degrees in your study with a group: sin, repentance, the Cross (the Gospel), and how to receive Jesus' victory into your walk with the Lord on a daily basis. Other issues are discussed fairly often, such as pride, lust, greed, staying away from alcohol, etc., but, because our flesh is so corrupt and will *quickly* run away from being crucified by faith in what Christ has done for us, we must always stay at the Cross. Think of it like this: if you were a cancer patient and you did not like the taste or feeling from the medicine you need to take in order to overcome the cancer, how foolish would it be to say, "Well, I decided today to stop taking my medicine, because I don't like the taste. And furthermore, I don't like the feeling as I take it!" The Message of the Cross is no different. Our flesh's loathing to admit we are wrong and that we need to repent does not mean that we should do anything other than that. Cleansing, forgiveness, restoration, and victory are all found in the Cross of Jesus Christ. Not the wooden beam to which they nailed Him, but the placing of our faith in His sacrifice for us, so we could have all the benefits He has provided for us. Remember that this Gospel Message is like one beggar showing another hungry beggar where to find food.

I have heard a number of "Bible teachers" make statements such as "we need to move on from the Cross to the meat of the Bible". My friend, there is nothing else to "move on" toward. If you do not yet realize that the Sacrifice of Jesus is the means of all blessings we receive, and the only way to be Sanctified daily, then you have overlooked or simply missed the Gospel Message in its entirety. The Bible study you teach needs to be centered upon the Cross.

If you know anything about basketball you know when someone has the ball and they are standing still, they, by rule, must have one foot planted. They can turn in all directions, but they must do so by pivoting upon that foot. Bible study and teaching is quite the same: you can head in any number of biblical directions, but what never moves and that upon which you must lean is the Cross. If you break this rule in basketball by simply ignoring it, it ceases to be basketball and becomes another game. If you break this rule in studying and /or teaching the Bible, it ceases to be the Gospel and becomes simply "religion".

There is nothing wrong with doing your best to make the atmosphere of the Bible studies relaxed and enjoyable. People bring soda, coffee, even snacks, at times, for everyone. In an outside church or home Bible study you may hear the leader say that they want no food at all, or even drinks. However, I believe that a relaxed study (not a service) helps for people to be more comfortable. Just make sure this does not become an interruption to the study in any way, a distraction.

Be aware and ready for this, though: no matter how comfortable and fun you make the Bible studies, there are people who will stop coming to them because of the Message that you teach. It is not because of you—although some will blame you at times—it is because many are looking for "religion"—something that makes them feel better about themselves—instead of desiring to be sincerely delivered from sin. The Message of the Cross brings them face to face with a choice in their lives: to either have their flesh crucified and be delivered from sin, or to run away and choose their sin and religion, instead of the blessing of God. It is only one way or the other, and most choose to run, so do not be discouraged when they do; simply pray for them and treat them kindly, even when they are slandering you and your ministry/study. Darkness hates the light, and the flesh must always try to kill the Spirit.

What I have seen in the Bible studies is the hearts and lives of many men changed. Those who have been faithful to the studies have grown in grace and knowledge. Despite their circumstances and trials, each man has matured in the Lord steadily, and their fruit is the evidence of that.

In addition to the Message on which the studies need to be centered, the commitment that the faithful make in coming to the studies holds them accountable to one another. You cannot be "sold-out" to the Lord, come to Bible study, fellowship with the Brothers, and live a lifestyle of sin at the same time. Something has to give, no matter how good someone is at playing games. The studies work for those who are serious, and those who are serious study the Message of the Cross.

Just recently a guard at the prison told me that their church held a study and the question was asked: "What is meant by being a disciple?" One person said it meant that you need to sacrifice some things. Another said something that the guard could not remember. The answers given had no impact on those who attended, and the guard who relayed to me the story still had no idea what the correct answer was. The truth is, today's church has no clue what it means to be a disciple of the Lord Jesus Christ. Most think it means to go around doing "good things" so people will like you as they believe people liked Jesus. This is as far from the truth as you can be, and simply man's "religion".

Here is what the Lord Himself said to us: *"Whosoever he be of you that forsaketh not all he hath, he cannot be my disciple"* (Luke 14:33)

And also, *"If any man will come after me, let him deny himself, and take up his cross daily, and follow me.*

"For whosoever will save his life shall lose it: but whosoever will lose his life for My sake, the same shall save it" (Luke 9:23-24).

What are we to forsake and deny? Ourselves and all we have! What does that mean? It means that we do not look to ourselves for the answers and power to overcome our problems; we look to the Cross of Christ.

Jesus did not go around doing "good things" so people would like Him. In fact, the "church" of His day hated Him because He exposed their phony religious ways. Being a disciple of Jesus today brings the same treatment from "the church". When you are "sold-out" for Him, which means you realize fully that the undiluted Gospel is the *only way* of victory, they will hate you, too. You will be so joyous over what the Lord has given you and the freedom you have in Him that nothing else will matter. This is what it means to be a disciple, and a follower of Jesus, and there are few who have chosen to take this direction. This is what your study needs to help others understand as you build them in the faith.

You have probably heard the term "the faith" at times. People misapply the term all over the world within what calls itself Christianity. "The faith" means only one thing: the Believer placing his faith in Jesus Christ and Him crucified. That is "the faith"! Do not accept anything different than that. If so, it becomes *"another gospel, another Jesus, another spirit"* **(see 2 Corinthians 11:4)** and eternal damnation in the judgment to come **(Hebrew 9:27)**

The Lord gave us a commission to *"Go ye therefore and teach all nations,... Teaching them to observe all things whatsoever I have commanded you: and, lo, I am with you always, even unto the end of the world. Amen. Preach the Gospel to every creature ... and that repentance and remission of sin should be preached in His name among all nations"* **(Matthew 28:19-20, Mark 16:15, Luke 24:47).**

When you do this, you will be teaching a Bible study correctly, and you will help men to be disciples of the Lord Jesus Christ. There is no other way. You will know that what you are doing is correct because the evidence of His being "with you always" will be the fruit you produce, which starts with changed hearts and lives of the men involved.

Running a Christian Library

There are a number of important reasons why you need to run your own library of solid Christian materials. To begin, the overwhelming majority of books that you will find in the prison's chapel library are of very little help. Most are written by popular authors who claim to be able to show you all there is to know about being a Christian. I do not mean to sound unkind, but most well-known "Christian authors" have not the slightest idea how to even have victory in their own lives, let alone be able to share with others where victory is found. If they knew, they would center their writing upon the Message of the Cross, the Gospel. Once a person truly understands that Message—and it is the only one that God has given us for Salvation and victory over sin—they lock onto it and hold it tightly. Once you taste the freedom it offers, you will want to walk in that freedom and tell as many others as you can.

Since you will not find much, if any, material written on this subject in the chapel libraries, your best choice is to accumulate material of this nature on your own so you can grow and help others to do the same. There is also a big push in the prisons to limit the amount of material that a chapel library can possess. The Bureau has put forth directives to "streamline" what can be on their shelves, which is another push by the enemy to try to keep any material that would actually help someone from coming into the prisons. A few years ago the Federal Bureau of Prisons put out a list of books and other resources that they "hand-picked" to be on the shelves for inmates. Our chaplain was told to throw out literally hundreds of books and items that were no longer "acceptable" by the B.O.P. standards.

In reality, none of this really matters. It is important, however, to be aware of in order to be able to see what the enemy is scheming (Satan, not the B.O.P.!), so you know how to better serve. Since there is very little good material on the compound where you are, the opportunity exists for you to use the books that you receive to help others.

As with everything in your walk and service to the Lord, if you are willing, God will make a way. Early on in my journey with the Lord I began to see how the more I surrendered myself, the more I was blessed. One of the areas in which I was blessed, was in receiving good Christian materials. God began to bless me through ministries of which I had never even heard. I began to read as much as I could so I could learn, and one of the greatest blessings was being able to distinguish what was good solid teaching, from what I call "fluff". The fluff books have interesting titles and covers, but you get no further along in your walk with the Lord than before you read them. Sure, some of these types of books make you feel good with all their promises and "sure-fire ways", but it is like revving up a car motor and never being able to put it in gear. These books take you nowhere!

When I found books from which I could really learn, I began to share them with others. Soon after I had a collection of these books, and some of which I even had multiple copies. I began to see something in all this: the Lord was giving me the opportunity to minister to many people through the library I started. People began to come to me from all over the prison to read books that I had. As well, as I had conversations with people, I was able to recommend and lend to them books on various subjects in which they were interested. This has been a huge blessing both to me and them.

Over time I have narrowed the variety of books and materials I have available, but there is still a large assortment. At any one time I have twenty or more books out on loan. At the risk of sounding repetitive, I need to say it; although there have been some excellent books that I have discovered, learned-from, and lent to others, the majority of them have been the ones available at J.S.M. The study guides are excellent for learning the Message of the Cross, and second only to the Expositor's Study Bible. For men who truly desire to grow in the Lord, these materials are the ones you want to get into their hands. In the back of this book I will list the resources that I recommend to you, as well as ways you can possibly obtain materials at discount or even free of charge.

Do not be afraid to write a ministry and ask what they can send to you. Just make sure that the ministry you solicit is sending you solid doctrine based upon the truth. You may not know at first, but as you get to know the Message of the Cross, you will see what is true and what is not. Pray for wisdom. *"If any of you lack wisdom, let him ask of God, Who gives to all men liberally, and up-braideth not: and it shall be given him."(James 1:5)*

Some of the very popular ministries out there today will quickly send you their books and materials as soon as you write them. However, you must be aware that most of what I have seen from these sources has not been good. Satan keeps his peddlers of lies stocked with material and money to carry out his devices.

Check the names of authors you read. If most people speak highly of them, let that be a warning to you. The truth is never popular. Find out if they are part of the popular deceptive movements, such as "Word of Faith" (also known as "Name it and claim it", "Blab it and grab it", "Confess it and posses it") "The Purpose Driven Life", Dominionism (also called "Kingdom Now"), Hebraic Roots, Calvinism, Seventh Day Adventists, or any other perversion of Christianity. Do not carry or promote/spread cheap imitations. Stick with materials you know to be good and solid. Even if there is something accurate in books or materials from these ministries, why would you pick through the trash just to find a piece of meat when you can go to a butcher (a good source).

When your library grows big, and you have more and more books out on loan, it becomes difficult, at times, to keep track of the books. People have a tendency to take them and let them sit unread. In the beginning I kept track of them in my head, but after a few years I would forget a book here and there and the person to which I lent it simply never returned it. It is best to write down every book you have, and to whom you lend them. It helps your ministry to recall who has which so you can ask the borrowers how they are enjoying the book when you see them. As well, record the date they received the book. This way if a month or so passes by you can check with the borrower as to when he will be finished.

This is how I do it: If I see after a week or two that the person has not mentioned the book (which usually they will if they are serious about growing in the Lord because the content of the books I carry are very powerful), I ask him how he likes it. If he says, "Oh, I really like it, and I'm almost done", everything is fine, and I give him more time to read. If he says, "Oh, it's O.K., but I really haven't had much time to read it", I say to him something like, "O.K., but just to let you know, I have a number of people who want to read that after you get done." This is a true statement because I always have people waiting on books. Many times they stop me and ask me to select a book for them because they are done or almost done with the one I gave them. So apply a little pressure to them to do one of two things: (#1) (You hope) read the book or (#2) to return it so you can lend it to others. You do not wish to rush people if you sense that they really desire to read it, but have been sidetracked. Simply let them know that the book is really good and that they will enjoy it very much as they read it.

Be prepared when starting your library. It will be a part-time job some days. Ensure that you always "go the extra mile" by being willing to take the materials to the readers if necessary. Your desire needs to be to get these books into their hands! Because many people are sluggish about doing things at times, you have to take the initiative to make things happen.

Let me assure you of this, however: this part of your ministry is a must, and you will be a blessing to many, many people around you because of your efforts. Not only have many inmates been blessed by reading the materials I carry, but staff members as well.

The truth is, because there is so much garbage printed today that poses as "Christian", when you get real Christian material in the hands of others, they do not even know what to do, at times. It is as if you turned on the light switch in their heads. You begin opening their eyes to things about which they never knew to be existent. For those who really desire to grow in knowledge and grace of the Lord, it will be like striking gold.

No matter how much knowledge you have, you can only be in one place at one time. Running a Christian Library is an excellent way to share with others what you know is true, while being able to do many other things at the same time.

The Christian Locker

What is a "Christian Locker"? It is probably called by various names at different prisons, but it is a supply of basic hygiene items to which the Brothers can contribute for the new people coming into the prison. As a young Christian just arriving, some Brothers reached-out to me with toothpaste, soap, shower slides, deodorant, etc., which was a great blessing to me. I had nothing, and was unable to go to the commissary that day. A few months later the Brother who kept the supplies moved to another unit and left me in charge of the locker. It so happened that my unit was the intake unit for the entire compound, so everyone who came into that prison initially stayed in my unit (cell block). They were then moved a few weeks later to another, permanent unit. This meant that sometimes, we would have ten or more men come into our unit at one time from the bus. To handle the needs of these guys was a big responsibility. While managing the locker was a bit overwhelming at first, I soon realized what an awesome blessing it was. The Lord was breaking me of my fleshly inclination to stay in the background and talk to new guys at a later date. I was forced to learn to approach people right away as they came into the prison, and I thank God to this day for the lesson. I became skilled at going right up to them and doing my job. That ministry taught me so much and prepared me for the ministries that God had in store for me later on. It reminds me of the story of David being placed in charge of tending the sheep, in order to learn to later care for God's people. I do not compare myself to David, but the learning principle is certainly the same.

A ministry like this, giving out needed supplies to new prisoners, may seem insignificant to many people. Most will think it beneath them to take on such a task. But let me assure you, what man calls insignificant, God calls service to Him. It was and still is a great honor to do the work that He has put before me, even something like handing out toothpaste.

You see, the ministry is not about simply giving-out supplies. It is an opportunity to reach-out to many people as they first arrive at the prison, before they become entangled in the nonsense prison offers. Even the ones who have already been to prison get to see the love of the Lord firsthand. It makes a difference!

I remember, one day at the rec. yard, while sitting on a bench with some other men, a man whom I did not recognize stopped to talk with a man sitting next to me. A few seconds later I heard him say, "I remember you; you're Brother Russell." I was little puzzled because I did not think that I knew whom he was. He was a middle-aged black man who was not in my unit. He then said in a very serious and grateful voice loud enough for all of us to hear, "I'll never forget you as long as I live. When I came to this prison I was in bad shape. I had nothing. My family could not send me any money before I got here, and I was really feeling bad. But you reached-out to me and gave me soap and toothpaste, some other things, and you got me a Bible. I will never forget you. Thank you so much!"

Touched as I was at that moment, I quickly did what I knew to be best: I deflected the praise and said to him, "My friend, I thank you for your kind words, but if anyone deserves the thanks, it is the Lord Jesus Christ. He is the One who provides all I've ever given, and who loves you so much." The sharing of the items I gave that man happened years before but it was still very fresh in his mind. I wondered a number of times after that how much struggle he must have faced in his life before that time. He was so grateful that someone would reach-out to him; it was as if I had given him something of great monetary value.

As he will never forget the day he mentioned, I will never forget what he said to me that day as I sat on the bench. It really opened my eyes to how many more people were touched as that man was.

Let me share with you some information that will help you run a Christian Locker effectively in your ministry. Firstly, let us look at what a Christian Locker is not: It is not for the purpose of simply giving supplies away. You do not use this to go around doing "nice things". It is not a supply of items from which the men at the prison can borrow if they run out of toothpaste, etc. It is not a loan to people. It is not for the purpose of making people feel they are obligated to come to Bible study or service. There are no strings attached to the items you give. They are gifts.

Here is what it is intended to be: a ministry that reaches-out to new people on the compound so the **Lord** can be glorified. You use the ministry to help them on a material level so you can show them the love of Jesus, and then use the opportunity to share the Gospel. It is a tool, like many others, of which you need to take advantage.

What inmates can you approach when they come into the unit? All of them. It makes no difference whether they profess to be Christian, Muslim, Catholic, Mormon, or other non-believer. Use this opportunity to show them true love and concern.

Here is what I do: When new guys come into the unit I let them first go to the officer to find their cell number, as well as to see with whom they begin to talk. Usually someone of their own race asks them where they are from and whom they "run-with", as it is called. As they begin to settle in a bit, I usually approach them and introduce myself and ask their names. I ask them if anyone has gotten them any hygiene items yet. I try to let enough time pass so that if someone from their state or gang is going to supply them with these things, they have a chance to do so. As I said, our job is not to give away supplies; it is to use the opportunity to share the Gospel. If someone else gives them hygiene items, then that is great. We still ask them if there's anything else they need, and supply what we can. Some are more excited over giving them a honey bun than the hygiene items! The point is, you want to help them see that you, a Christian, care about them. You then use that to build the relationship.

Some people will be thrilled to meet you because they are a Christian also, and others will give you various reactions. I have found that almost everyone will be at least thankful for your kindness, whether they accept items or not.

Take advantage of your conversations with these men by letting them know who you are, your cell number, or where your bunk is, and that if they need *anything* they can come to you; that if they want a Bible you will find one for them; that you hold a Bible study to which they are welcome to come, etc.

Make an assessment of the men's reactions to what you say. If they seem very interested in a Bible, the studies, etc., spend some time with them as soon as you can. *Do not allow the enemy to tempt them into heading into a bad direction because you never followed-up on them.* If they do not seem very interested in seeking the Lord or Bible study, then treat them very kindly anyway and offer your help. You never know when someone is going to come to their senses and surrender to the Lord. You do not ever want to be a stumbling block to someone because they do not respond the way you prefer them to.

As far as stocking-up on supplies so you can execute this responsibility, you may at first have to purchase some things on your own. If you have some faithful Brothers around you, ask them to donate supplies so they can be a part of this ministry and blessing, also. Keep enough supplies on hand for five to ten people in case you get a large group. Better to have extra than run-out.

One very important piece of advice: be sure the supplies that you and the Brothers buy for the Christian Locker are the best that you can get; items that you would use for yourself. If you are going to bless someone, do not do it halfway. Do not buy the cheap products that no one else wants. Get them name brand items that are high quality. Jesus did not give us second best, and neither should we give second best.

The Christian Locker is what you make of it. You can turn it into a fabulous way to draw people to the Lord. Be creative. Never worry about how they react when you approach them. The Lord will be with you.

You will be amazed at how many people around you who watch what you do in ministry will tell you what a great thing you are doing. Especially the "religious" people because they see real love in action— something that their beliefs cannot offer. There is no real love in religion because it can only be found in Christ. Use those opportunities to reach-out and show them the love of the Lord. Share with them what Jesus has done for you in your life. Remember, no matter how "religious" they are, they cannot dispute your personal testimony.

There are times when you will see someone in need in the unit or somewhere at the prison. Use discretion. If you feel that your lending or even giving someone something from the Locker will further the Gospel, do so. Just be sure that you are the best steward you can be with God's possessions. And that is to whom they really belong.

Section II: Other People

New People

As I previously mentioned, new people to the prison can be swayed in a negative direction very quickly. I have found that, at first new people are a bit nervous because they are at a new location and they do not really know what to expect. After offering them supplies from the Christian Locker, they are very attentive to what you are saying, with many even asking for a Bible or inquiring about church services and Bible study. Unfortunately, most will very shortly find and join those on the compound who have no interest in serving the Lord. Do not be discouraged if men tell you one thing and, soon after, do another. This is common. What you need to do is treat them with love and sincerity, trusting that the *LORD* will bring them to Him at some point later on down the road. Always leave the "door open" for them. Never leave them with the impression that you are "judging them" because they did not stick to their word by not showing-up to a study, etc. That is not being effective in ministry.

For those men who do take steps forward in the right direction, you need to nurture them. Do not pressure them, but extend yourself to them so they have a good experience, overall.

Remember!—*"**People may not remember exactly what you did or what you said, but they will**"* *always remember how you made them feel." (Author unknown)*

Make yourself available to these new people. This may require some sacrifice on your end, but this is your opportunity to minister. They may require only a few moments or perhaps some extended time. If you are unwilling to be a friend to them, there are plenty of others who are more than willing to lead them into sin. The first few weeks are very important as far as overall direction they will go while they are at the prison. Do your best to be there for the people; offer them good materials to help them grow; share some food with them; let them see the joy and Christ-like character that is in you so they are drawn to the fellowship of Believers, not the quick pleasures of sin which will destroy them.

Letter Writing

The ministry of letter writing is one that often is overlooked by Christians in prison. Most Christians write and tell someone they love that something, a change, has happened in their lives, but most stop there. You have to realize that when you are in prison you have quite a bit of time to read the Bible, pray, fellowship, etc. People on the outside are caught-up doing their day to day running around, working, etc. God has given you a time-out in life to take you away from the distractions of the world. This offers you an opportunity to minister to those you know through letters. Do not underestimate the power of this type of ministry. Do not allow the enemy to whisper in your ear and say, "They'll never believe you! They'll think you just have jailhouse religion!" That's a lie. People take notice to changes that occur in others. If they begin to see or hear about real changes in your life they will want to know more. Many of them may be struggling with issues in their own lives. Use this to share with them the only cure for their problems, the Gospel!

Here is my suggestion: make sure in your letter that you stay away from anything that sounds as though you are putting them down, and, as well, be very careful how you word things if they are involved in religion. You do not wish to have your words interpreted as though you are attacking them or their religion. People are very attached to their religions, so you have to be wise in how you share with them.

Along with not being able to dispute your personal testimony, it is very difficult for people to deny God's Word when they read it or hear it. Many do, but they have to really perform a lot of self-deception to manage it. The point is, when you share with them God's Word, it will always have an effect. It may not work as quickly as you would like, but here is what the Lord said:

"So shall My Word be that goes forth out of My mouth: it shall not return unto me void, but it shall

accomplish that which I please, and it shall prosper in the thing whereto I sent it." (Isaiah 55:11)

As well, never be ashamed of sharing God's Word with anyone. The results of witnessing are not your responsibility. God handles that part, as only He can. If there is any doubt about the effect remaining, here is what God says:

"For the Word of God is quick, and powerful, and sharper than any two-edged sword, piercing even to the dividing asunder of the soul and spirit, and of the joints and marrow, and is a discerner of the thoughts and intents of the heart." (Hebrews 4:12)

The Word of God is effective on its own. Your job as a servant and minister is to share His Word with others in the best way possible. That means making sure that when you write people (or talk to them) you allow the Word to be offensive, if in fact that happens, NOT YOU!

Do not demean them; do not be overly pushy; do not send a letter that is a sermon from the start to finish; this will "turn them off". Your letters need to up-lift them and to let people know God's power and love for them, not to have people dread reading them. You want to encourage people and share with them the changes that have taken place in your life so they begin to see how real Jesus is. That is not to say that you do not mention sin, repentance, the Cross, etc., but simply be wise in how you share.

I have found that the ministry of letter writing has been a powerful blessing to those whom I have written, as well as to myself. And to be quite frank, writing is not my favorite exercise. I enjoy communicating, but I do not look forward to the actual writing process. However, it is necessary! If you are not efficient at first, make it your goal to become proficient. Ask the Lord to help you in this area *("James 1:5").* Developing your writing skills will pay-off very well for the ministry in the future. Being able to communicate through words or by letter is extremely important in ministry but it takes a willingness, effort, and persistence. You cannot fail unless you never try. Do not worry about how the letter sounds at first, just begin to write.

In your prison ministry you must have contact with ministries on the outside. This, too, requires good communication skills in your letters. I learned early that there are some wonderful ministries that are very willing to help you serve the Lord while you are in prison. All you have to do is write some of them and see what help they offer. Some will send books, some monthly publications, some pamphlets, etc. These tools are excellent help in your ministry. Just be sure that the ministries from which you receive materials are preaching the truth, which is the Message of the Cross, the Gospel.

There is a list of sources which I recommend at the back of this book.

Pray for Those Who Ask for Prayer Right Away

When you are known as a true man of God in the prison, the people will begin to come to you and ask you to pray for them and/or with them. This is a great honor. You must never let these opportunities slip away. If they live in your unit/cell block, step into your cell or some other place where you can go, and pray with them right then and there. People are deeply touched by this. They are grateful that you would do so. Perhaps not knowing the Lord themselves, they look at you as a connection to Him. Use this to build your relationship with them and to introduce the Gospel to them. When the Lord gives you an opening like this, use it!!

As well, there will be times when someone stops you on the rec. yard or on a walkway (or wherever) and shares with you something they or someone they care about is facing. Do not waste time! As they say, "strike while the iron is hot". Pray with them right there and then! Do not ever worry about what others may think. Many a man wishes it were him with whom you were praying, but he is too scared or proud to ask to do the same for him. You may find that others may even come to you as a result of seeing you pray for someone else.

As I have said earlier, when one man has the boldness to stand up and trust the Lord, others will follow. Praying for others is an excellent way to help others see the power of God show-up in their lives, as well as opening their eyes to His love and care.

Family and Loved Ones on the Outside

For those who have loved ones, friends, etc., on the outside, you need to realize that for some of them you may be the only Christian with whom they either come in contact or to whom they are willing to listen. This is a tremendous opportunity for you to make a difference in their lives by not only sharing with them the Message of the Cross, but also allowing them to hear/see the changes that have taken place in you. Those who knew the "old you" also know that some serious changes have taken place, especially if you were heavily involved in the vices of sin and have now been delivered. It is tough for others to deny the power of the Lord when they see a dramatic change in someone about whom they care.

Here is where it gets a little tricky, and I hope through this section I can save you the mistakes that many others have made, including myself.

As young Christians, those who have had a powerful, life-changing experience that *we know* is real, we become really excited and we want to tell our loved ones what happened. There is nothing wrong with desiring to tell everyone about what Jesus has done for you, but using wisdom in doing so is key to being effective. You must understand: the fact that you now know the Lord does not mean they understand all that has happened, and some will not even be interested in hearing about it. Yes, they care about you, but unless you use caution in what you say and *how often you say it,* you will do much, sometimes, to turn them away from the great blessing you have received, rather than draw them closer to Him. As I mentioned in the section on letter writing, you do not wish to have all your communication to them simply about the Bible, repentance, etc. These are loved ones who are there for you, not someone you have encountered who is asking you about your faith because they are seeking. This is not to say that your loved one may not be seeking, as well, but you must not be overbearing. In your desire to do something good, you can easily offend someone who loves you because you are not using wisdom.

When I was very young in my walk with the Lord, I, without realizing what I had been doing, pushed loved ones away from me because I could only see things from my point of view. I was not meaning to offend anyone, but that is what I did. I was not being led by the Holy Spirit; I was being led by myself, my flesh. It does not work. It took years to repair the damage done during that period, and to get them to once again listen to me about spiritual matters. Just because God is doing a work in you, you ought not to assume that it is His timing to do the same work in others. Do not push! Surrender your life to Him fully, and allow Him to work in you so you can then be prepared to lead them to the truth. Do not mistake their love for you as an automatic sign that they want to hear you talk about the Bible, their sin, how they need to go to church, etc. Take things one step at a time, with the first step being the focus on the Lord cleaning you up. Your loving them deeply, openly, and unconditionally will do more than all your talk.

"Preach the Word always: if necessary, use Words!"

Being Wise While Standing Up for What is Right

As a Christian in prison you will see many things transpire that are not good. People try to take advantage of one another constantly; they prey on others, cause intentional harm, etc. You cannot get in the middle of everyone's battles, nor should you. It is not your place to do so. However, there will be times when you will see a person who says he is a Christian—whether you see the evidence of that in his life or not—who runs into some problems with unbelievers. Perhaps he did something to bring about these problems, or perhaps it was a result of bad circumstances. You have to look at the situation and make a judgment call as to whether or not you need to get involved or not, and to what extent, if necessary. A person who claims to be a Christian but lives a lifestyle of sin cannot expect his "brothers" to come to his aid because he cannot pay his gambling debt or alcohol debt that has now caused him a major problem. One thing for sure: as quickly as a Believer can spot someone who is not what he claims to be, the world can spot it faster. The world will even bow down to "religious people", but they look for ways to expose a false Christian, as well as anyone who has simply fallen into sin. There is nothing wrong with showing mercy and grace, but your job is not to bail out of debt those who refuse to repent of their sins!

Warning: In your desire to be involved and to see the right thing done, you must be aware of several potential dangers. Firstly, you must always realize that everything you say to others can and will be used against you often. You may tell a person that he is in danger and that his best option is to "check in" (go to administration and be placed in the S.H.U./hole for his personal safety), and he will use your name while doing so, thereby putting you in danger of getting locked-up because of your care for him. As well, some men that you will advise will take your words, twist them, and tell others a completely different story. You must expect these types of persecutions, and use foresight and wisdom at each step. Do not put yourself in unnecessary danger with staff or inmates by assuming that your good intentions will be interpreted as you meant them or that the individuals you assist will be heart-set on your better interests. Be prudent. Guard what you say and do. Trust in the Lord and never overlook the possibilities of the danger a person may cause you.

There will be at times, as well, where the unsaved will begin to gossip about a Brother. The less time a Believer spends in fellowship the easier it is for this to happen. Things turn ugly at times, even to the point of mobs forming against someone. This is the time you need to go to the Lord and pray, if you have not already done so. If you feel you are being led by the Holy Spirit to get involved (not by your flesh!), then do so. However, remember that in all your dealings with opposition you must use wisdom, and remain humble and gentle. If the Lord has told you to get involved, or you simply know it is the right thing to do, then proceed, but do so cautiously. Do not allow your emotions to tangle things up! Remember that the wrath of man does not work the righteousness of God.

Not too long ago we had a situation occur where a young guy in his mid-twenties came to the prison and said he was a Christian. He was here about two weeks but really showed no desire for fellowship or to be part of the services, Bible studies, etc., offered. He seemed a bit nervous at times, also. Soon after, the wicked began to talk about him. Before long he was labeled as a pedophile, although no one looked at his actual charges. Word got back to us that a large group of individuals were going to attack him one night. The question was, "What were we to do?" Were we to simply let "the world" take care of its own problems, or were we to get involved even though we saw no evidence of his being a Christian? These are tough situations in prison. You may be made aware of these things as they go on, but your job is not to run and tell the administration. Not only do you put yourself in harm's way, but your testimony to the lost will be destroyed. You have to use wisdom from the Lord. *(James 1:5)*

In this particular situation, we thought it best even though we would be going against a mob of at least two-hundred or more, who were on one accord in their evil intentions, to try our best, a group of only a handful of us, to bring about peace somehow. We knew, at that point, that the young guy with the problem could not make it here, so we thought it best to try to get him off the yard without incident. That meant we had to go to the main people who were behind the mob, and try to talk some sense into them. One of the risks you run by doing so, in a case like this, is to be labeled as someone who sticks-up for child molesters. Regardless of whether or not the accused was involved in something like that, if we did not proceed with the Lord leading the way, and very cautiously, this is the backlash that we would be facing. We were not looking to poke a bee's nest, only to bring about peace.

In the end, the kid left the yard with only a few bumps. His own resistance to listening to reason cost him those bumps because he tried to play hardball when he should have humbled himself and used the opportunity to go while there would have been no problems. We did our job—what we thought was right—and we had no regrets. Some people were upset at us for a while, while others developed new respect that they had not had before the incident. It took courage on the part of all the Brothers involved. It was not easy. But God was with us to see us through.

Pray about situations like this. You cannot do it by yourself, nor are you called to. God is not glorified on your part by your taking matters into your own hands. But when He sends you forward and you obey, He will be with you. You need Him involved in all aspects of your ministry, and things can turn ugly in prison very quickly when situations like these arise and you try to handle things yourself.

Be wise. Pray. Be obedient to the Holy Spirit's leading.

Opposition and Persecution You Will Face

As a servant of the Lord who teaches and stands up for the truth, the Message of the Cross, you can expect much persecution. The unbelievable part is not that you will, but from whom. Expect the vast majority of your opposition and persecution to come from what calls itself "the church". There are those who will stare the truth right in the eye and call it a lie. They will oppose you and all you do for the Lord (what God does in and through you). Why? Because darkness hates the light. Your light and the truth that you preach expose the evil to which they cling and which they protect. The "church" is filled with false brothers who not only hide-out there, but try to use it as a platform to control others. They are fake and phony, and usually have large followings. Nothing is more insulting to the Lord than someone's calling himself a Christian while standing for evil. Remember, the root of evil is pride. Pride breeds those in church who are bogus and counterfeit, both leaders and their followers. The leader tells the followers that he has the answer to all their problems, and all they have to do to receive what he has is to bow down to the false leadership which he provides. It is no different than when Satan said to the Lord, *"**All these things will I give You, if you will fall down and worship me** (Matthew 4:9)* Our answer needs to be the same to them, *"Get Behind me Satan"*.

Some of your opposition will be very subtle, and some will be blatant. Both arise because of opposition to the truth, but some put on a better face. Here is how you will know who stands with you or against you: If people center their beliefs and teachings on the Gospel of the Cross, and you see love evident in their lives, then they are with you. If not, they are in opposition to you (and God), whether they know it or not.

Over time you will succeed in winning some of these men to the truth, but it will be very few. The roots of religious pride run quite deep. Do not be surprised when those you thought were with you are found to be playing both ends against the middle. Always choose your words very carefully so you give as little ammunition as possible.

I have found it a losing battle to think that you can get all who are steeped in religion/false doctrine to see the truth. If you spend some time with people and they still reject what you say, then move-on. The Word says, *"A man who is an heretick after the first and second admonition reject; knowing that he who is such is subverted, and sins, being condemned of himself."* **(Titus 3:10-11)**

It is never a pleasant thing to do, but you, as a Believer, must stand against the teachings of the wolves that have come into the church, posing as Brothers, and men of God. It is also unfortunate that, at times, many who you would like to trust, including the chaplains, will not stand for the truth, but will in every way support false teaching and those who bring it forth. Do not let this discourage you. Continue to do what is right/best, knowing that God is with you.

I have come to understand this: there are very, very few people who will ever truly serve the Lord. If you are blessed enough to have a handful of Brothers who are "sold-out" to Him, then praise the Lord. Most people are content with what they have, and Salvation is no different. As long as folks have the assurance of it, they rarely move forward from there. Remember, the battle belongs to the Lord. Draw closer to the only One who can help you; Jesus. Do not let the imposters draw you into their arena, and do not let them sidetrack you from your work. The enemy is very clever. If he cannot get you to follow false doctrine, he will try to get you to chase after worthless distractions for the sole purpose of wasting your time.

Here are some scriptures that will help you better understand and deal with the men who claim to be Christian but promote false doctrine, and whose aim is to control others (see **Nehemiah 6:1-4**).

"For they loved the praise of men more than the praise of God." **(John 12:43)**

"Take heed therefore unto yourselves...for I know this, that after my departing shall grievous wolves enter in among you, not sparing the flock. Also of your own selves shall men arise, speaking perverse things, to draw away Disciples after them. Therefore watch..." (Paul's final words to the Ephesian elders. **Acts 20:28-31)**

"This know also, that in the last days perilous times shall come..men shall be lovers of their own selves...lovers of pleasure more than lovers of GOD; having a form of godliness, but denying the power thereof; from such turn away...ever learning , and never able to come to the knowledge of the truth...but they shall proceed no further: for their folly shall be made manifest unto all men..." **(2 Timothy 3:1-9)**

"But there were false prophets also among the people, even as there shall be false teachers among you, who privily shall bring in damnable heresies, even denying the Lord that bought them, and bring upon themselves swift destruction.

"And men shall follow their pernicious ways." **(2 Peter 2:1-2)**

"For the time will come when they will not endure sound Doctrine; but after their own lusts shall they heap to themselves teachers, having itching ears;

"And they shall turn away their ears from the truth, and shall be turned unto fables." **(2 Timothy 4:3-4)**

"Beloved, when I gave all diligence to write unto you of the common salvation, it was needful for me to write unto you, and exhort you that you should earnestly contend for the faith which was once delivered unto the Saints.

"For there are certain men crept in unawares, who were before of old ordained to this condemnation, ungodly men, turning the grace of our God into lasciviousness, and denying the only Lord God, and our Lord Jesus Christ." **(Jude 3-4)**

False Doctrine

Most who have studied the Bible to some extent will be able to see with ease/immediately that the false teachings of the world's religions are based upon false doctrine. These are fairly easy to spot when you know what God says, and usually have a few common denominators, such as teaching that Jesus is not God, that He did not die on the Cross (or a cross!), that your salvation is dependent upon your works, etc., plus many, many more that space will not allow to be listed. We know these to be false so the chances of our following after them are unlikely. However, loads of false doctrines are taught by many who name themselves Christians, and are accepted by millions. Here is just a few of the *false* teachings that are very popular and believed by many in the church today:

(1) <u>Word of Faith</u>

> This lie of Satan's has convinced millions that they are little gods who possess the same creative powers as God Himself, and that all one must do is confess scriptures he selects that apply to what he wants, and begin to believe them. The focus then becomes the person's own will, not the Lord's will for that person's life. A big part of this lie is the supposed miracles and healings a person will be able to perform, all the while staying away from the subject of sin, which is

taught by these blind guides as being a "bad confession".

Many volunteers who preach and teach at prisons follow this lie and spread it to eager "confessors" who focus their attention on how quickly they can confess their way out of prison, and thereby taking them out of God's will for them at the present. This particular lie is very appealing to the religious prisoners because of its false promise of superiority among the others they are around. If nothing else, this doctrine does an excellent job of exposing those who serve themselves from those who serve the Lord.

(2) Oneness Pentecostal

This popularly deceptive movement claims there is no Trinity, or Father, Son, and Holy Spirit being three separate persons. Its promoters claim that God is one person who appears at different times in different forms or modes. In other words, sometimes He is God the Father, and sometimes He is Jesus, etc.

The emphasis of this cult is doing works and keeping laws they themselves have invented. Within their network there are groups who believe various falsities, but most share some common lies such as: men must be clean shaven and have to wear long sleeved shirts (even white only); women cannot wear make-up, jewelry, and must have long hair; one must speak in tongues to be saved, etc.

(3) Calvinism

This tangled perversion of God's Word teaches its followers that God is a very cruel creator who refuses to extend mercy and grace to people who could be saved but instead go to Hell for "His good pleasure". It is a lie that has been successful in convincing prideful men that they are one of the "chosen ones" or "elect" that God prefers over others. This deception is a slap in the face to God who loves all men very much, and *"wishes that none should perish but, but all come to repentance"* **(2 Peter 3:9)**

The Bible says that *"God so loved the World"*, not simply a few select people. Calvinism also teaches the false doctrine of "Once Saved, Always Saved", or what is also called "Unconditional Eternal Security."

(4) Purpose Driven Life

This powerful deception is the creation of a man who is now called by many, "America's Pastor". This fact alone shows the spiritual blindness of our country today, accepting anything that simply calls itself "Christian".

The Purpose Driven movement is also based upon works, but this worldwide push is aimed at bringing people of "all faiths" together in unity to make the world a supposedly better place. Very popular in prisons, this lie teaches its followers that the answers are found in doing the author's 40 day program, not in the Gospel of Jesus Christ.

The Purpose Driven Life bases it's deception on verses taken from a book called The Message, which claims to be a Bible version, but is, in fact, a mockery of God's Word.

There are many, many other popular deceptions today that the "church" follows after. There are too many to list. As a rule of thumb, if it's popular, chances are there is something wrong. The world and the flesh do not praise the things of God.

Dealing With Problems Between Brothers

This issue, like all others, requires wisdom for correct handling. Problems will arise, so it should be no surprise when it happens. The important thing is not that a problem occurs, but how it is handled. Surely we would like to never see problems surface between

Brothers, but since we cannot stop them, we need to deal with them in the best way possible.

Most issues happen because of pride. The Word says, *"Only by pride comes contention."* **(Proverbs 13:10).** If you can understand this, the whole process will be much easier, especially defusing tension. If you have repeatedly taught about the sin of pride and how to overcome it with others in the Bible studies, then its ugly face will be that much easier to recognize.

Most of the time, disputes can be settled if someone with wisdom will simply talk some sense into one or more of the Brothers involved. However, if you are not on one accord, it becomes very difficult. For example, if there is a problem with a Brother or Brothers who say they are Born-Again Believers but really seem to be religious, then the pride that is usually involved (on their end) makes it very difficult to reason with them. Remember, not everyone who claims to be a Brother really serves the Lord. Most of what calls itself the church serves itself. There is very little humility. You have to recognize before you deal with an issue whether or not you are working with people who are humble enough to receive from you. Few are actually willing to do the right thing, which always begins with true humility. Do not be shocked when you see men who claim to be learned, Spirit-led followers of the Lord, acting in ways that contradict all they profess to believe and love.

The Bible says *"Blessed are the peacemakers"* : and although that firstly means those that proclaim the only way to peace with God, the Gospel Message, it also includes those who strive to bring peace to a potentially evil situation.

What I have found to be effective in dealing with problems between Brothers is this: to begin, do your best, no matter who seems to be right or wrong at first, to treat each individual impartially and with respect. The appearance of a situation at first can be deceiving, and as well it adds fuel to the fire when someone perceives you as taking a side. Remember, in the end it rarely matters even what the problem was, the important thing was how the people involved handled themselves and treated others. If your relationships with Brothers begin to deteriorate, your relationship with God has probably deteriorated. Let God fix your relationship with Him by humbling yourself and surrendering to Him, and you will find favor restored not only with God, but also with men.

Take the time to talk to those involved if you are able to do so. If the men have developed a respect for you and they trust you, they will usually open up to you. Be very careful in what you say because, during the time of a problem, things can easily be misinterpreted, and people are easily offended by even neutral parties.

Many times the approach you take will be determined by how well you know the individuals. If you know them well, you can be more "to the point". Those who do not know you very well may require a little proving of yourself to them in showing them kindness, sincerity, humility, and concern.

Once you are able to talk with someone openly, and they receive from you, ask them to share with you, their side of the story. *Listen to them.* Do not interrupt people, simply listen, and if you need to ask some simple questions to understand one side of things, such as "then what happened?" etc., then do so. Be sure your body-language and facial expressions are ones of concern and interest, not of displeasure, or anything that can be taken offensively. Regardless of how you feel about what someone has done, be the best friend you can to both parties throughout the process and afterward. Again, the incident will almost always "blow-over" and be forgotten. What will not be forgotten is your treatment of folks at this critical time. However you treat them, they will remember, so be sure to act with love and wisdom as a minister of God.

Without sounding judgmental or preaching at them, try to bring the conversation to the Lord, and how He would desire "us" to handle the situation. Use the words "us" and "we" to ensure a Brother does not feel like an outcast and alone. Do not forget: the goal is repentance, and it is usually needed in all parties involved. One side may have "started it", but the other side many times responds wrongly and hurtfully.

Although Christians are supposed to be loving, kind, forgiving individuals, living lives to the glory of God, in actuality, most of these men, particularly in prison, are vain, proud, petty juveniles who care more about what people think about them than what God thinks. This is wrong; however, it is the sad fact. In order for you, a peacemaker, to ease the process (for bickering children!), you must try to help both parties to "save face". This means to help everyone involved refocus on the Lord and their priorities, which do not change simply because they perceive someone to have sinned against them. Our first priority is always to be our relationship with God (see the first commandment, **Exodus 20:3**, also **Matthew 22:37-38**). The second priority is to selflessly love His children, our Brothers and Sisters in Christ (see **Matthew 22:39**). When you do this, you give them opportunity to "break away" from the fighting, tension, etc., without appearing to be weak or cowardly. The truth is, neither one most likely wish to be involved in the altercation/dispute, but once tempers have flared, and that "ol pride" is in play, a good ending will probably only be brought about by the Lord making peace through one of His servants, as you are called to be.

"Depart from evil, and do good; seek peace, and pursue it: (**Psalm 34:14**) (See also: **Matthew 5:9, Romans 12:10, and James 3:17-18**).

If a person is honest, he will admit his fault and that his actions were wrong in the Lord's eyes. If you can get both sides to humble themselves, you have made progress. If only one, it is still a start. Be sure you tell those who are willing to repent that they are doing right by the Lord, but remember to always do so without looking as though you are taking a side. When the problem is finally resolved, your impartial stance will have played an important role. You will have built more trust in all parties, and they will be much more inclined to listen to you in the future.

If someone refuses to humble himself when he is wrong, you cannot do it for him. Pride is a beast to handle. People know when they are wrong; you do not have to repeat it again and again. You can, at times, remind them of their responsibility to the Lord, as well as the cost to them as they remain stuck in their pride (rebellion), but it is best that you allow folks to cool-off if they are upset before you share things with them.

Problems do not happen by accident. Most times it is fairly easy to see what the Lord is trying to reveal to us, in ourselves and in others, if we are just willing to look. I cannot stress enough how much of the problem will be pride, and the solution being to humble ourselves. When others look to you for leadership and answers, you must be humble, impartial, attentive, compassionate, and be able to lead them in the right direction, which is always to the Lord and what He did for us at Calvary.

Problems, I have found, are really opportunities to glorify the Lord and help those involved to grow. They are not easy to defuse most times, but can be used to our advantage, if we allow that to happen, by obeying in faith.

Exhorting and Rebuking

There are times when you, as a Brother and a leader, need to rebuke those who are in error, or exhort those who need to be warned. Here is what the Word of God says:

"Rebuke a wise man, and he will love you" and *"Open rebuke is better than secret love. Faithful are the wounds of a friend; but the kisses of an enemy are deceitful: (Proverbs 9:8; 27:5-6)*

To rebuke someone means to reprimand or reprove, which means, in our case, to correct someone sternly, but with love and always with a correct motive. Inside the parameters of being obedient in faith, our motives need always to be doing so because it is in that persons best interest, not simply because we are upset with them, which may also be the case. The Bible says that *"Fools despise wisdom and instruction"* **(Proverbs 1:7)**, but a wise man will take correction from others, even openly, if need be, because he values God's Righteousness over his pride. A wise man prefers to acknowledge his errors, receive instruction, and adjust his thinking and behavior, than continue in his folly in order to maintain the pretense/appearance that he is never wrong.

Be wise in how you handle these situations, doing all you can to minimize the offense. Be discreet. Do not correct men in public if that is not absolutely necessary. If you make a person feel as though he is an idiot in front of others, when the situation could have been handled differently, he will resent what you have done and likely not receive from you. Your purpose is not to embarrass someone, but to correct him when necessary *so he learns*. Be sure *you* do not hinder the process/progress by being thoughtless (inconsiderate), or offensive in something you do personally.

People may be upset with you at times when you tell them they have done something wrong, but if you approach people with the right motive, attitude, and in a spirit of love and meekness, they will learn to appreciate what you have done for them.

The same is true for warning others. Brothers will take steps in certain directions to see where that path leads. When you know that these paths are not beneficial to them it is your job to exhort them, which means that you give them urgent warnings and encourage them to take the correct path. This may not be what they wish to hear, and many will be stubborn enough to ignore your warning, but you will have done your job. As well, whether rebuking or exhorting people, you need to make it clear that you are not rejecting them as a person, but coming to them because of their action. You need to make it clear that your rebuke or exhortation does not imply that you have turned your back on them. Express to the men your hope of seeing them do the right thing, whether that means repenting or changing what they are doing, or both.

You will find at times that people will respond to you with, "who are you to judge me?" This is the response of an immature Believer who is still unwilling to repent and surrender his sin. Do not let this type of response faze you; simply explain that we are called to judge within the Body of Christ, and our judgment needs to be a righteous one that stems from the right motive, which you are practicing. Paul said, *"do not you judge them who are within?"* meaning that if someone calls themselves a Christian, they are considered to be "within" the Body of Christ , and therefore subject to judgment by mature, Spirit led Christians. Not to be judged in motive, or to condemnation, but to have their actions judged according to the Word of God. (See **John 12:48)**

It is not a pleasant task to correct someone. At times it can be very difficult and draining. When you know that your actions are right in the Lord, then good results will follow, and –we hope—soon. This type of work is taxing, and your only source of refreshment is found in the Holy Spirit. He will give you all you need if you depend on Him. Remember, the Holy Spirit only works in our lives to the extent He desires when our faith is found in the finished work of Christ. The Cross is where we find our direction, our strength, our comfort, our rejuvenation, and all we need to accomplish the tasks the Lord places before us. As Brother Swaggart rightly said, "it is the Cross, the Cross, the Cross!!"

The correct order of the steps in modifying the behavior of a professing Believer to the standards in God's Word are as follows; pray, instruct, correct, mark and dis-fellowship. (Note: prayer is needed between each step, as well). In prayer, the first step, you must ask the Holy Spirit to prepare *your* heart (see **Galatians 6:1**) and be sure you remove the log out of your own eye before you address someone else's flaws. Secondly, pray for the Lord to humble the person to receive instruction and correction, and prepare his heart, otherwise you may as well talk to the wall, because he will reject what you are saying, or reject you and what you are saying. The fact that you observe mistakes, errors or behavior which brings shame to the Gospel and the glory of God, etc., or even that you are prompted by the Holy Spirit to address this issue, does not mean that here and now is the time to do it.

The second step, instruction, is teaching the difference between right and wrong, wisdom and folly, knowledge and ignorance, etc., for unlearned Believers. The Word of God says, ***"All scripture is given by inspiration of God and is profitable for Doctrine, for reproof, for correction, for instruction in Righteousness: That the man of God may be perfect, throughly furnished unto all good works."*** **(2 Timothy 3:16-17)**. This means that you are not instructing people on the sole basis of your life experiences, but you are being used by the Holy Spirit to explain (clarify) the scriptures. (see also **2 Timothy 2:24-26**).

The next step, correction, involves numerous means of adjusting someone's beliefs or behaviors to conform to God's commands, sound doctrine, etc. Both the instruction and correction are the responsibilities of the Holy Spirit; He often utilizes mature Believers as instruments to which the young Believers can relate. The forms of correction vary in severity depending on the conditions. Some of the factors to consider in choosing the proper approach are: the extent of the damage and its ramifications, the level of development of the Believer in the faith, the overall maturity of the person, how public the sin is, etc. Once you have taken all of these elements into prayerful consideration, the Holy Spirit will guide you in how to proceed. Be discreet and wise; always approach humbly. If you are perceived as "holier than thou", judgmental (condemning), condescending, compassionless, etc., not only will you be poorly received, but you will give the person being corrected an excuse to dismiss the message with the messenger. People should feel like help has arrived when you show-up, not their grade school principal whom they despised. Approach the person with authority, but with tenderness and compassion. Remember, the goal is accomplished in your demonstrating God's love and concern for the person, and God's desire to restore the person's proper relationship to God, which is conditional upon his repentance.

When the person acknowledges his sins and repents, encourage him heartily, and validate his decision. Be sure to explain to him how pleased God is when we, as sinners, humble ourselves and repent of the sin, thereby allowing the Lord to wash, heal, and restore us. Remember, repentance is what God expects from each of us. He knows that you are going to sin. As soon as you realize you are sinning, God wishes you to run to Him so He can clean you up, as only He can. Do not let guilt interfere with your turning to Him, as the enemy would like to have happen. Since Jesus already dealt with your sin two-thousand years ago, His concern is not your sin, per se (the particular act), but your heart and willingness to repent. What is necessary is the response of your heart and your willingness to repent. Remember, it is not the actions of the sin you have committed that concern God so much as it is the rift (separation) that it causes in your communion/fellowship with Him. When correcting a Brother or Sister, you must explain this fully. Be sure your attitude, both toward the sin and the sinner reflect God's attitude. This can only happen if you are being led by the Holy Spirit; His ability to work through you in this capacity is dependent upon your faith's being properly placed in the finished work of Jesus at Calvary, and your confidence in God's desire to use you and to restore the person.

Keep in mind, as well, that in the prison setting, you are dealing with men who are very image-conscious/insecure/proud. Make sure you consider the most effective approach for each individual when correcting him. If you can, get him alone with just you and perhaps someone else whose advice he will accept and heed. This will make it easier to lower his defenses and lose the 'hard-guy' image. No one likes to be publicly reprimanded.

Dis-fellowship

To dis-fellowship from an erring and unrepentant Brother or Sister is one of the most difficult tasks in ministry for which you will be held accountable by God. Because you live in close proximity to one-another in prison, sharing a table in the chow hall, or even a cell, breaking fellowship can be a very awkward and uncomfortable obligation. If you both attend the services at the chapel, you will continue to encounter him after taking this step of obedience.

God has given you a very clear pattern of behavior as a gauge or measure to recognize His true disciples. Love will be the most evident trait, but, also, joy, peace, humility, and other fruit of the Spirit. (see **Galatians 5:22-23, John 13:34-35**). People who regularly display behavior that is inconsistent with Godly conduct, and embrace a worldly lifestyle of sin, are either unsaved or rebellious. You cannot love both God and the world (see **Matthew 6:24, 1 John 1:15-16**). When you see that a professing Believer's walk does not match his Sunday talk, you have the responsibility of correcting his behavior. If your loving correction is refused, and he chooses a lifestyle of sin (see **Matthew**

18:15-17), advise the erring Brother that if he will not repent of his sin, he will leave you no choice but to shun him until he does. Make it clear to the person that you do not dislike him or consider yourself to be better than he is, but God commands His children to be separate, holy, sanctified, consecrated, etc. Understand the Bible truth that *"A little leaven leaveneth the whole lump"*. Sin spreads if not treated as the cancer it is. Because sin separates us from God, Who is life, it brings death. Sin does not just affect the person committing the sin, but all the people around him. If you really love God, sin will be offensive and disgusting to you. Any man who continues in his rebellion and refuses your help must be put away from the Body before his evil spirit infects others.

Religious people, especially those in leadership positions, will not understand or appreciate your stance on separation because their goals are not God's goals. They seek to extend their influence and reputation to as many people on the compound as possible. For those of us who *"seek firstly the Kingdom of God and His Righteousness"*, *"straight is the gate and narrow is the way, that leads unto life, and few there be that find it"* (See **Matthew 6:33; 7:14**). When you are teaching the Message of the Cross, and separating yourself from people who do not live the Gospel Message, you will be in opposition to those who court popularity. While they are seeking to gain a larger and larger following, and compromising with heretics and hypocrites to accomplish this, we seek the acceptance of God and not the approval of men, especially the ungodly!

While your character is being attacked and slandered by the men whose hypocrisy you are exposing, for your uncompromising obedience (in faith), expect also that they and their pawns will come to you with one of the biggest lies in Satan's arsenal: "We all just need to come together and put our disagreements to the side. After all, the Body of Christ is not divided, and neither should we be. You are only causing division in the Body by what you are doing."

Let me be clear so there is no misunderstanding: We are not to come together in unity; we are to come together *IN TRUTH!!* We do not unite the true body of Christ with a harlot!

"You adulterers and adulteresses, know ye not that the friendship with the world is enmity with God? Whosoever therefore will be a friend of the world is the enemy of God." (James 4:4).

People who are willing to befriend the world, under the banner of "unity" or any other such nonsensical excuse, are the enemies of God and His Gospel. The Body of Christ *is not* divided; in this they are correct. The point that they refuse to acknowledge is that those who will embrace the world are not part of the Body; they are the enemies of God.

As you live-out your Message of repentance and separation, your popularity will nosedive. Pretty soon the only people who will appreciate your sincerity and truth will be sinners and outcasts (publicans and harlots!), and, if you are fortunate, a few dedicated men who take up their cross daily to follow Jesus. *(Luke 9:23"*

People in the church love to point their fingers at others and say, "you are the problem", when clearly they're the ones who serve themselves, not the Lord. The division comes when you, "the troublemaker" refuse to go along with their religious, ungodly ways. Here is what the Word tells us to do with these people, also:

"Now I beseech you, brethren, mark them which cause divisions and offences contrary to the doctrine which you have learned; and avoid them.

"For they that are such serve not our Lord Jesus Christ, but their own belly; and by good words and fair speeches deceive the hearts of the simple." (Romans 16:17-18)

Even if you are the only one on the compound who loves God enough to separate yourself from the world and religious pretenders, do not get entangled in endless arguments and debates; simply withdraw yourself and live your life of separation so others will *"see your good works and glorify your Father in Heaven"* (see **Matthew 5:16**). Pray for the Lord to send people to you who are truly seeking Him, and avoid any fakers who will waste your time. If you are walking in fellowship with the Lord, pleasing Him and not men, the true seekers and real Brothers will recognize your genuineness and will be drawn to the Spirit they see in you.

The Lord directs you to separate from the world in two particular ways. God's people, firstly the nation of Israel, and now the church, are commanded to actively separate (sanctify, consecrate, be set apart) themselves from the world, and to reserve themselves for Him. Also, you as an individual are called to separate yourself from anyone or anything that degrades your relationship with God, or directs your focus from God's will to your own desires. The collective/group separation is traditionally called "Ecclesiastical separation", which derives from the Greek word "ekkalein" (ekklesia) which means "to call forth", "summon". God has called us to come forth from the world to Him through Jesus, by faith.

Personal separation, unlike corporate, is primarily directed to preserve the individual from distractions, such as fools, scorners, scoffers, and carnal Christians who would hinder a Believer's growth. Ecclesiastically, we separate from "religion" and the values of the world, primarily a doctrinal separation, whereas, personally, we separate from influences and temptations. (See **2 Thessalonians 3:6** concerning bad behavior and **1Timothy 6:5** concerning bad doctrine).

I suggest that you do not rush into taking strong action in regards to an individual or a group, but I suggest that you pray for guidance, and do what is right in the Spirit of the Lord with His leading. Let the Spirit of God show you what needs to be done, and why; act accordingly. If, after separating yourself from someone, you see he is repentant, then praise God and welcome him with open arms. Your purpose is never to toss anyone away, but to follow the Word of God and trust for the repentance of the prodigal son (daughter).

Once again, I remind you that dis-fellowshiping is never an easy process, and can be very taxing, but you must keep in mind that you remove bad apples, not because you despise them, but for their own good and preservation of the good apples. Turn to the Lord for your strength. He is there for you.

One final note: your disposition, the way you treat the person you are disciplining, will likely be a deciding factor in whether or not he repents or seeks the company of Christians again. Far too many people have rejected the Body of Christ on account of the bad attitudes of its members. Remember, but for the grace of God, there go you. You never know when the shoe will be on the other foot, and you will need correcting. Treat the person as you wish to be treated, as Jesus treats you. Be humble.

The Prison Chapel, Chaplains, and Those of Other Denominations

Prison chapels are places where people from various faith groups gather at times to study and worship. Because so many groups exist, usually the different faiths are assigned specific times to hold their services. I have seen Brothers become disgruntled over having to share the same room throughout the week as other faiths, although at different time slots. You must understand that the chapel is open to other faith groups. In fact one of the biggest mistakes that I see Believers make is failing to use the time at the chapel to witness to other groups. You may begin this process by being kind and considerate to the people who are there from other groups, and building upon that. Who would want to be a Christian if all they ever see and experience from Christians is an unfriendly attitude towards them? If I were lost I would think that Christianity is all about looking-down upon others and being uptight. Unfortunately, incidents of this nature happen all too often. Do not let this happen. Reach-out to the lost. Show unbelievers the love of Christ. So what if they do not believe what you believe? The only way to convince them to lower their guard and listen to the truth is to show them that you care about them and are sincere.

Much of how the chapels are run is dependent upon the leadership of the chaplains. In fact, the old saying "Everything rises or falls upon the leadership" holds especially true when it comes to evangelizing and discipling. If there is good leadership where you are, you will see good fruit produced. If not, you will see bad fruit.

In my time in the federal system, I have met some wonderful chaplains who have a real heart for God's people, and have used their position as a chaplain to minister to the prison population. They have not worried about "policy", although they proceed wisely, but kept in mind that one day they will have to give an answer to the Lord Himself for their actions. *(Matthew 12:36)* If you are blessed enough to be around one or more of these types of men, then be sure to thank and praise God for them continually. Having a chaplain with a heart for God's people is a great asset to the prison, as well as to your personal ministry. Your goal should be the same as his: win souls to Jesus, and make disciples of them afterwards. If this in fact is your common objective, then you should be able to work with the chaplains in achieving this. Despite your denominational beliefs perhaps being different from theirs, so long as the chaplains are not proponents of false doctrine (major issues), you should be able to work together as a team. This may require patience and understanding if either of you are a little "rough around the edges", but every effort should be made to work together and be on one accord; one accord in faith and truth, that is, and nothing short of that. When I say "major issues" of false doctrine, I say this because we can still strive towards a common goal alongside others while in prison, over-looking minor differences in our beliefs. In fact, the more grounded we are in our knowledge of the truth, the easier it is to help these others to see for themselves.

Dealing with those who do not believe exactly as we ourselves do has been a problematic issue, especially in a prison setting where all "Christians" usually join together for one singular service. How are we to interact with these Brothers, and where do we draw the line and separate ourselves from them? Firstly, we must have a common belief that the Gospel is what saves, not our own works or anything else. We must agree that *"by grace are you saved through faith; and that not of yourselves: it is the gift of God. Not of works, lest any man should boast."* (Ephesians 2:8-9)

Here much wisdom is needed on your part. There will be *many* who claim to agree with this, but few whose lives exemplify this belief in action. In other words, many will call themselves "Christian" but their lives say otherwise. Many will agree that we are saved by grace through faith (they have a tough time denying this verbally!), but will spend their time trying to work their way into God's favor, and attempt to teach others to do the same.

If you see good fruit in someone's life, such as love for souls, a hatred for sin, particularly his own, and an overall love for the Lord, then work with him, even if you know he does not subscribe to the same denominational belief as you. I am not saying that you even ought to claim a denominational title, but if you are

226

a Christian, you *will* be lined up with a known denomination, whether you admit this or not. So if someone who loves the Lord is Baptist, and you are a Pentecostal, focus on what you have in common; do not nit-pick over your differences. You cannot change him, only the Lord can. Reach out to him in love, not criticism. Let your love help lead him to the truth of God's Word.

Getting back to the chaplains, I must warn you that I have seen/met/interacted/worked with some horrendous ones, as well. I have dealt with men who, while claiming to be leaders and men of God, support the works of the enemy, and allow false doctrine to be taught and preached in the Christian community, even after having been warned by myself and others repeatedly.

Listen to me carefully: there are many wolves in sheep's clothing. A man's calling himself a Believer, or having the title of chaplain, preacher, or minister, does not mean that he serves God. You are under no obligation to sit at the feet of someone who does not stand for what is right. In fact, when you do so, you are actually putting your stamp of approval upon his teachings and ways. This does not mean that you reject someone each time you do not agree with him, but it means that you examine his teachings and his work. You are going to know a lot about a man by the way he treats God's people.

If you have a chaplain who gets sermons off the internet when he preaches, there is a problem. He probably needs to get saved, and you need not feel that his standing before a congregation requires you to support such "leadership".

Remember this: when two or more are gathered together, you can have church. It is better to worship with one true Believer, than one thousand fakes. Have church in your cell if that is your only option. If you see the problems, some others will as well. It only takes one man with bold zeal to make a difference. Just be sure that you are not acting prematurely, or out of your flesh. Seek the Lord about this and every other important decision you make. Most decisions really are important, even if they seem insignificant.

The chapel, if led by men of God, can be a real blessing to many when excellent preaching, teaching, and counsel are available. As well, programs such as classes to help make men into disciples, classes on Evangelizing/Defending your faith, etc., can be a real boost to the Christian community. The goal for all Believers should be to do the will of God, and a major part of that should be winning souls to Christ.

In many chapels there is an assortment of videos available to be viewed. Some of them can be informative and entertaining with such stories as Abraham, David, Jeremiah, etc. There is also much garbage in many chapels. Many videos are deceptive and either blatantly or secretly misinform the viewers! You have to be careful.

Prison chapels usually have a variety of reference materials, as well. These materials, including commentaries, concordances, Bible dictionaries, books that translate Hebrew and Greek into English, etc., are very useful to Believers. Become familiar with them and put them to use. They will help you in your personal growth, as well as your Bible studies to help others.

Section III: Help for Your Ministry

Materials You Will Need

To make things easy I will list materials which I recommend that you obtain both for you and your ministry.

1. The Expositor's Study Bible --- This Bible is by far the best available today for understanding scriptural application. None of the other popular, well-known Study Bibles focus on helping the reader understand spiritual truths and applications of those truths to your spiritual life. They are primarily sources of historic, cultural, geographical, and biographical facts. The ones I have seen that deal with spiritual applications, have, for the most part, been very poorly informed and mistaken in the teaching they put forth. The Expositor's is easy for beginners to understand, but deep enough to teach the veteran scholar.

2. The Cross of Christ Study Guides – These treasures put into simple, easy-to-read terms such subject as: The Sin Nature, God's Prescribed Order of Victory, **(Romans Chapter 6)** How the Holy Spirit Works,etc. If you desire to grow spiritually, these study guides are a must-have.

3. <u>Jimmy Swaggart Bible Commentaries</u> – these commentaries, unlike others I have seen, and I have seen *many*, are easy to understand while digging deeply into the scriptures. They not only explain the original Hebrew and Greek, but they tie everything together and show you how the Word of God is applicable to the Church today. The comparisons of the early Church and its growth and problems to what we face today as Believers, exceed any other works I have discovered. Do not overlook these rich resources.

4. <u>Jimmy Swaggart Books</u> – These easy-to-understand books will show you, by the use of the scriptures, the answers to many questions you will have in regards to the Cross, leading a victorious life in Christ, Bible doctrines, and frequently asked questions. They are a must-have for your Christian Library.

5. <u>Books by Dave Hunt and T.A. McMahan</u> – Over the years I have benefitted greatly from the writing of these wonderful Brothers. I strongly disagree with their beliefs on Unconditional Eternal Security and the Baptism in the Holy Spirit, but I recommend their writings, anyway. These Brothers have been an excellent source of information on the deceptions in the modern church. Straight

and to the point they never hesitate to sound the alarm when they spot the work of the enemy, both inside and outside the church.

6. Books by Albert Dager (Media Spotlight)
   Brother Al has written a number of books that address topics (deceptions) in the church that need to be known by all who profess Christ today. Thorough and well documented, this Brother does an excellent job at taking apart and exposing Satan's repackaged schemes.

7. Books by Mark Cahill
   At this printing this Brother has two books available in both English and Spanish. When it comes to sharing your faith with others, Mark Cahill is the one to read. His proven ways are very effective, and his second book, One Heartbeat Away: Your Journey into Eternity is a book that even people with tough objections to Christianity have found to be enlightening. This is the kind of book you can give to someone who is not sure what to believe, and have confidence that if he reads it, he will have come face-to-face with the truth of who Jesus is, as well as his desperate need for a Savior.

8. Newsletters and Monthly Publications
   The following monthly free newsletters/magazines will be of great

value to the man of God who has a ministry.

A word of warning: Because something is offered for free, there is no guarantee that it is good. The prisons are flooded with materials from very popular but deceptive ministries that will quickly send free magazines and books. Most of them promote/push the ungodly "Word of Faith" teaching, which men, desperately looking to get out of prison, embrace quickly. You can depend on the publications I listed above to be Gospel centered.

A. The Evangelist- Sent free from Jimmy Swaggart Ministries, this magazine is extremely informative and will help educate you in the Word, as well as show what is currently deceiving the churches.

B. The Berean Call --- Dave Hunt and T.A. McMahon's dynamite free newsletter that exposes Satan's tricks, as well as gives the readers many answers to common questions.

C. Media Spotlight --- Al Dager offers the Body of Christ a wonderful free publication that gets right to the heart of current and reoccurring deceptions. An asset to every Believer, and past issues are made available by title.

D. <u>World Challenge</u> --- This sermon, sent to subscribers for free every three weeks, is always a refreshment to readers. This Spirit-led ministry is now carried forward by Gary Wilkerson.

There are many fine books that are available to help build Believers in the Faith, as well as for teaching how to reach-out to the lost. I want to be very clear, though, regarding my recommendations: simply because I recommend someone's book, newsletter, or other materials, does not mean that I agree with all they teach. You need to "search, the Scriptures daily to see whether those things are so" (see **Acts 17:11**). My suggestion is that you pray about everything and seek wisdom from the Lord when looking at the teaching of others. If an author is telling you that there is an answer to sin outside of the Cross of Christ, discard it promptly. Do not be afraid to throw a book in the trash if it is promoting something that is not biblically correct. I have read some excellent books from certain authors, and then found some of their other writings to be way off in some area.

9. <u>Tracts</u> ----- As I have previously said, tracts can be an excellent way to share your faith with those with whom you come into contact. There are a few publishers that produce interesting tracts which are very "catchy". People love to read these, and they get the readers to think about their sin, their lost condition, and the only solution to it all: the Cross of Christ.

Source List

1. Jimmy Swaggart Ministries- PO Box 262550, Baton Rouge, LA 70826
   Phone: 800-288-8350

2. The Berean Call- PO Box 7019, Bend, OR 97708   Phone: 800-937-6638

3. Mark Cahill- PO Box 81, Stone Mountain, GA 30086 Phone: 800-638-7158

4. Media Spotlight- PO Box 290, Redmond, WA 98073-0290

5. World Challenge- PO Box 260, Lindale, TX 75771

6. Chick Publications (tracts plus much more) PO Box 3500, Ontario, Canada 91761-1019 Phone:909-987-0771
   http://www.chick.com

7. Living-Water Publications-(tracts)Phone: 1-800-437-1893 http://www.livingwater.com

Radio and Television

By far the most powerful, life-changing radio and a television station available to the world is Son-Life Broadcasting. You may not be able to watch this where you are, but if possible you need to listen to the radio stations.

Have your chaplain contact **Chaplain John C. Bayer at Free at Last Ministries P.O. Box 84501, Baton Rouge, LA 70884.**

Trusting the Lord for Materials

As with everything in your ministry, you must seek and trust the Lord for all you need. In all my time in prison I have *never* seen someone go without his needs being met if he was truly seeking God and His Will. When a man surrenders himself to the Lord, and commits to serving Him, God will provide ALL he needs. This includes materials for your ministry. **"My cup runneth over". (Psalms 23:5)**

God is not going to call someone into ministry, and then not provide for them. Humble yourself and seek His leading.

Remember, the Lord will be working with you, and as Jesus Christ is lifted up ---- He will draw all men unto himself.

Conclusion

The Biblical and practical truths found in this book are intended to inform, instruct, educate and assist you in your walk as a Christian in prison, and/or if you feel called by the Lord to start a Christian Ministry on the inside. Many, if not all, of the daily activities of prison life are covered in detail from a Christian perspective.

I sincerely hope that the information in this book has been and will continue to be informative and instructive. My prayer is that the Lord, by His Holy Spirit, will embed the truths and practical application of those truths into your heart and life, and that you may be able to walk in them as you minister and nurture those whom the Lord sends your way.

Remember, yourself as well as those to whom you will minister, will become,

"His workmanship, created in Christ Jesus unto good works". "Ephesians 2:10"

Russell Nestor

Salvation Prayer

Dear God in Heaven, I come to you in the name of Jesus, I acknowledge to you that I am a sinner, in need of a Savior, and I am sorry for my sin and the life I have led. I believe your only begotten Son Jesus Christ shed His precious blood on the Cross at Calvary and died for my sins. I am now willing to turn away from my sinful life and start living for you. I am ready to be saved. You said in your Holy Word.......

Romans 10:9-10 "That if you believe in your heart that Jesus Christ is the Son of God and that God raised Him from the dead, you shall be Saved, for with the heart man believes and with his heart confession is made unto Salvation".

Thank you Jesus for your Grace and Mercy and your precious blood that was shed for my sins. I thank you Jesus that your Grace never leads to a license to sin, but rather, it always leads to repentance. Therefore Lord Jesus, transform my life so that I may bring Glory and Honor to you all the days of my life and not to my self. Thank you Jesus for dying for me and giving me eternal life.

Amen!!!

If you have prayed that prayer and sincerely asked Jesus Christ to come into your heart and be the Savior and Lord of your life, them please write us and tell us of your commitment to Jesus and we would love to send you your Spiritual Birth Certificate. Our mailing information is found in the back of this book

Chaplain John

Prayer for the Healing
of my Past

Heavenly Father, thank you for giving me Your gift of Salvation, Jesus Christ. I come to you now in the mighty name of Jesus and I give you my past. I know it is covered in the blood of Jesus and it is cast into your sea of forgetfulness and that my sins are as far as the east is from the west and never to be brought up against me again.

I ask you Father, to heal my memories, to remedy the wrongs of my past, and to turn my past into something that can be used for good in my future and the future of others. I choose to give up my claim to my past and turn it completely over to Jesus Christ.

Through Your Holy Spirit help me forgive myself and put the past behind me forever.

Thank you that I am a new creation walking forward into my future in and with Christ. I pray this in the Precious and Incomparable Name of Jesus!!!

Word From Chaplain John

If you just prayed that prayer and truly meant it with your whole heart, you are saved and all of Heaven is rejoicing to one sinner who repents.

Now please go to your Bible study leader, prayer partner and your Chaplain, tell them of your prayer and your commitment to serve the Lord.

Please write us and tell us of your comments on our book and that you prayed the sinner's prayer as you were led by the Holy Spirit. We welcome your comments and may use them in our other publications as we feel they may benefit other readers.

Remember God will never leave nor forsake you, He loves you unconditionally, you can do nothing to make Him love you any less, nor can you do anything to make Him love you anymore.

Christianity is not about you working in God, but about God working in you.

Your position in Christ is not based on what you do, but on what you Believe. For you are His workmanship, created in Christ Jesus.

Acknowledgement

Donations to this ministry will help provide this publication to chapels and prisoners throughout the country and more.

Free at Last Prison Ministries, LLC
A Non-Profit 501 (c) (3) corporation
P.O. Box 84051
Baton Rouge, Louisiana 70884

www.freeatlastprisonministries.org

Any and all contributions for the furtherance of this labor of love for the Lord, would allow us to continue our efforts and accomplish this mandate set before us in a manner pleasing to the Lord.

"Always about our Father's Business"---"Preach the Cross, to the Lost, at any Cost"

"Your Gifts are Tax Deductable"

What Inmates Have to Say

"I am currently serving a 120 month sentence in a Federal Prison. I have been here for five years now and I have experienced firsthand, as well as seen many, many lives changed for the better through Brother Russell's ministry. Take full advantage of what is taught in this book if you truly desire to serve the Lord while you are in prison (or elsewhere), and I assure you that you will be blessed."

Brother Tom M. Hatcher

"Through my years of being in prison I have seen all types of books, but none directed toward prisoners, nor on how we can have a successful ministry from within prison. As I typed this book, I learned a lot from it. The Lord has used this Brother powerfully, and this book will be one of the most useful tools any Christian can possess in prison or at home." *Brother Michael Baker, Ex-Inmate*

"What this book teaches is what changed my life. I highly recommend this book to prisoners who want to serve the Lord, or to just anyone who desires to learn the Message of the Cross, the only true Gospel." *Brother Victor Velasquez*

"This book was a real eye opener for me, and made me rethink a lot of my own thoughts, feelings, and motives. I saw with my own eyes the differences in the men, before and after. It isn't just "Jail-House Religion"! I follow many of those who've been released, and the changes stuck. Their lives glorify the Lord, which is the evidence of good teaching. It lifts up Jesus, who loves, heals, and forgives.

Brother James Wing, Ex-Inmate